INSTANT ACTIVITIES
FOR CLASSROOM SUCCESS

Over 100 Creative Curriculum-Based Activities

by

Dorothy Michener & Beverly Muschlitz

Incentive Publications, Inc.
Nashville, Tennessee

Edited by Sally Sharpe

ISBN 0-86530-095-X

Table of Contents

Preface vii

TIME FOR THINKING

School Bus Know-How *(Following Directions)* 10

Our Flag *(Following Directions / Using rhyming words)* 11

Signal Words *(Understanding Signal Words)* 12

It's For The Birds! *(Critical Thinking)* 13

Horsing Around *(Reasoning)* 14

What Next? *(Sequencing)* 15

Babbit The Circus Clown *(Creative Thinking)* 16

Video Mania *(Problem Solving / Logical Thinking)* 18

Focus On Success *(Setting Goals / Making Schedules)* 19

A Day At The Zoo *(Following Directions)* 20

REASONS FOR WRITING

On The Right Track *(Learning Process Writing)* 22

A Class Yearbook *(Writing Articles)* 23

Poetry For Two *(Using Rhyming Words / Writing A Haiku)* 24

Ballooning *(Writing Poetry / Visual Imagery)* 25

Write Stuff *(Writing About "Me")* 26

Check It Out *(Proofreading)* 27

In The Beginning *(Writing Creative Stories)* 28

Sarge *(Writing Creative Stories)* 29

Wise Bird Word Puzzles *(Using Picture Clues)* 30

Lennie The Helpful Lightning Bug
   (Sequencing / Determining Sentence Order) 31

My Delightful, Descriptive Paragraph *(Writing Descriptive Paragraphs)* 32

Where On Earth Would You Go? *(Writing About Chosen Topics)* 33

Welcome To The New School Year! *(Writing Letters)* 34

Hats Off To You! *(Recognizing Skills & Accomplishments)* 35

Your Astrological Sign *(Using Research Skills / Writing)* 36

STIMULATION FOR READING

A Is For Author *(Authoring Books)* 38

Going Bats Over Halloween *(Reading & Following Directions)* 39

Three Kids And A Dog *(Reading Comprehension)* 40

_____ Loves This Book *(Writing Simple Book Reports)* 42

Real Or Make-Believe *(Distinguishing Between Real & Make-Believe)* 43

Stellar Speller *(Reinforcing Spelling Skills)*..44

You Can Do It! *(Reading & Following Directions)*..46

Mother Goose Lost *(Finding Missing Words)*..47

Motivating The Reluctant Reader *(Reading Motivators)*..48

Thumbnail Sketch *(Writing Brief Book Reports)*..50

Magic Carpet Report *(Writing A Book Report)*..51

Bookmark Awards *(Reading Motivators)*..52

CLUES FOR COMPUTATION

Not Too Late *(Telling Time)*..54

Bunny Money *(Adding Coin Values)*..55

Sweet Tooth Bakery *(Matching Numerals & Number Words)*..56

Code 9 *(Working Addition / Subtraction Problems)*..57

Halloween Problems *(Working Math Problems)*..58

Computer Headache *(Solving Magic Squares / Number Puzzles)*..59

Topsy Turvy *(Reinforcing Math Skills)*..60

Holiday Problems *(Finding Addition & Subtraction Equations)*..61

Emily's Farm Fun *(Reinforcing Addition & Subtraction Skills)*..62

Valentine Problems *(Working Math Problems)*..63

Coupon Roundup *(Reinforcing Math Skills — Group Activity)*..64

Otto's Auto Maze *(Recognizing Multiples Of Six / Multiplication)*..65

Dragon Math *(Working Math Problems)*..66

Apple Al's Orchard *(Using Math Operations)*..67

The Super Deluxe, Please!
   (Solving Addition / Subtraction / Multiplication / Division Problems)..68

Spring Problems *(Working Math Problems)*..69

Chef's Corner *(Understanding Fractional Parts)*..70

Timbo The Clown *(Working Math Problems)*..71

Brain Quizler *(Solving Math Problems)*..72

PROMOTING HEALTH AND SAFETY

Strangers Good And Bad *(Learning About Good & Bad Strangers)*..74

Health Helpers *(Recognizing & Understanding Health Helpers)*..75

Trisha's Tonsils *(Understanding Health Problems)*..76

So Where Is The Tooth Fairy? *(Learning About Teeth & Dental Hygiene)*..77

My Weekly Exercise Log *(Keeping An Exercise Log)*..78

Have A Better Breakfast Week — Give Your Train Go Power
   (Reinforcing Good Eating Habits)..79

Food For Thought *(Learning About Nutrition / Making Wise Food Choices)*..80

Bicycle Safety Check *(Understanding Bicycle Safety)*..82

When Things Go Wrong *(Understanding Feelings)*..83

Differences *(Appreciating Individual Differences)*..84

Litterbug Walk *(Expressing Environmental Concerns)*....................................85

All-Star Safety Student *(Recognizing Safety Precautions)* 86

Magic Words By Professor Hare *(Improving Human Relationships)*.............87

The Enemy *(Learning About Good Eating/Exercising Habits)*......................88

Clowning Around Can Be Fun *(Learning About Acceptable Behavior)*.........89

Tell Us What You Do Well *(Developing Healthy Self-Images)* 90

A Healthy Me From A To Z *(Reinforcing Good Health Habits)* 91

Have A Safe Halloween
   (Understanding Halloween Safety/Finding Hidden Words) 92

INSPIRATION FOR FUN AND GAMES

Mind Your ABCs *(Reinforcing The Alphabet)* 94

Star Gazers *(Developing Creative Thinking Skills)* 95

Buddies, Pals And Friends *(Conducting Interviews)* 96

Time For Re-Leaf *(Encouraging Creativity — Leaf Projects)* 98

The Gingerbread Race *(Reinforcing Various Skills — Game Board)* 99

The Sleepy Giant *(Developing Listening Skills — Game)* 100

Seasonal Outreach *(Decorating The Classroom — Patterns)*....................101

Play Call Ball *(Developing Listening Skills — Game)* 102

Crazy Cut Ups *(Writing Creative Stories)* 103

Join The Proud Crowd! *(Reinforcing Positive Self-Concepts)* 104

Puddle Jumpin' Rainy Day Nonsense *(Solving Riddles)* 105

Invitations *(Communicating — Reproducible Stationery)* 106

Parent Summer Plan *(Involving Parents In Summer Planning)* 107

TIPS FOR CREATIVITY

Boxy Art *(Making Box Projects)*..110

Dictionary Mobiles *(Using The Dictionary/Creating Mobiles)* 111

Seasonal Scoop *(Creating An Announcement/Display Board)* 112

Look Of The Month Club *(Creating A Student Work Display Album)*.........113

Monkey Capers
   (Decorating The Classroom/Providing Creative Activities — Pattern) 114

Photo Finish *(Using Photographs For Creative Activities)* 115

Shapely Art *(Assembling A Puzzle/Spatial Relationships)*........................116

Belonging *(Creating Back-To-School Bulletin Boards)* 117

Families At Home *(Learning To Get Along With Others)* 118

Sunny Side Up *(Communicating — Reproducible Parent Letter)* 119

Creating The "Healthful" Classroom *(Meeting Student Needs)* 120

Look At That! *(Making A Telescope/Developing Observation Skills)*..........121

Blurbs, Blurbs, Blurbs *(Learning To Write Blurbs)* 122

Pets, Pets, Pets *(Learning To Take A Survey)* 123

Achievement Awards *(Reinforcing Positive Self-Concepts)* 124

Rebus Recipe (*Writing Rebus Stories*) 125

On The Road Again (*Developing Creative Writing Skills*)....................................126

Extinct Means Forever (*Bulletin Board Idea*) 128

Alternative Energy (*Demonstration Of Solar Power*) 129

Seasonal Critters (*Reusable Patterns*) 130

Conservation Worksheet
    (*Learning That Conservation Begins With Appreciation*) 132

The Flying Squirrel (*Learning About Unique Animals*) 133

Willie The Whale That Lost Its Tail (*Creative Writing*) 134

Save The Roos (*Learning About Kangaroos*) 135

Air Everywhere (*Learning How Air Helps Us*) 136

Eye On The Sky (*Learning Cloud Types*) 137

Bits And Pieces (*Mini-ideas For The Teacher*) 138

Environmental Calamity - Help Our World Take Action!
    (*Conservation Bulletin Board*) 139

Be The Solution - Not The Cause (*Demonstrating Recycling Awareness*)..........140

Panda Puzzler (*Panda Word Maze*) 141

All About Whales (*Whale Statistic Word Maze*) 142

Litter Hunt (*Developing Litter Awareness*) 143

Stop! You Are Hurting My World
    (*Learning About Endangered Or Theatened Species*)...............................144

Adopt A Sea Mammal (*Resources For Adoption Programs*) 145

Aquarium Antics (*Planning An Underwater Habitat*) 146

Trashy Story (*Learning About The Problems Of Trash Disposal*) 147

Where Have They Gone? (*Identifying The Special Needs Of Living Things*) 148

Some Creatures Make You Smile (*Categorizing Animals*)..................................149

Our Protectors (*List Of Environmental Organizations*)......................................150

Sal The Puppet Gal And Sam The Mitten Man (*Suggestions For Puppetry*) 151

Happy Sal The Puppet Gal, Sad Sam The Mitten Man
    (*Hand Puppet Construction*) 152

The Color Green (*Fostering Nature Appreciation*) 153

Wilderness Conquest (*Gameboard Learning*) 154

Shuttling Above And About (*Super Challenge Writing Composition*)..................155

Glitter - Don't Litter (*Taking Action To Fight Litter*) 156

Headwork And Footwork
    (*Science Experiment - Discovering Sources Of Pollution*) 157

Making Fog And Smoke (*Demonstration - Making Fog And Smoke*)...................158

Wilderness Conquest (*Variety Gameboard Cards*) 159

Answer Key..160

PREFACE

Teaching is a special field, indeed — a truly important occupation. Teachers do, in fact, mold the lives of future generations. Yet, so much of what a teacher accomplishes is determined by the individual. Principals, school districts and states have their standards and requirements; however, it is not necessarily *what* one teaches but *how* one teaches that makes the difference. That's what this book is all about!

INSTANT ACTIVITIES FOR CLASSROOM SUCCESS is a collection of ready-to-reproduce-and-use curriculum-based activities designed for use with elementary students. All of the activities have been developed so as to be easily modified or adapted for differing ages and capabilities. One activity, for example, might be equally appropriate for an average first grader and a learning disabled fourth grader. Feel free to adjust the activities as necessary to meet your specific classroom and student needs. Thought-provoking activities for more capable students also are included and may be identified by the label "Super X Challenge."

The activities and ideas in this book may be categorized as teacher pages or student pages. The teacher pages may be identified by this symbol:

Each teacher page contains a teacher-directed lesson, activity or "just for you" tip or idea to help simplify daily teaching.

The student pages are intended for reproduction and may be identified by this statement: © *1990 by Incentive Publications, Inc., Nashville, TN.* Many of the activities are inter-disciplinary and provide for the reinforcement of various skills. Attractively illustrated "blank" student pages also are included to allow you to create your own "tailored" activities. Simply add the appropriate activity or instruction for your class.

In addition to teacher and student pages, reproducible game boards are provided to give you an additional fun way to reinforce skills. Some of the game boards have themes and others are "open-ended." Select the "content" and prepare the game boards for the students, or let the students complete the game boards themselves.

Because this is a success-oriented book, many of the activities have no one correct answer. This allows students to complete activities without worrying about the grading process. Regardless of how a student completes an activity, his or her work has value.

Although education is "serious business," it need not be dull. This book provides you with creative, "success-oriented" activities that will delight students and enliven your classroom. So, down with drudgery and up with creativity!

CHAPTER 1

TIME FOR THINKING

School is often threatening to students because of the grading process. The activities in this chapter will provide opportunities for individual thinking as well as reinforce skills.

So often activities have only one correct answer or response. However, a number of the activities in this chapter are open-ended, encouraging students to think independently and to make choices. For example, "Babbit The Circus Clown," "It's For The Birds" and "Horsing Around" allow students to make varying responses.

Asking students to share their ideas is an important part of learning and should be encouraged. The slow or timid student should be helped to recognize that he or she has something worthwhile to contribute. Whatever the student's response may be is "OK."

When there is no right or wrong answer, the pressure is off and success is built into the activity!

Name _____

SCHOOL BUS KNOW-HOW

Follow these directions carefully.

1. Color and cut out the pictures of the people.
2. Paste the driver in the seat behind the wheel.
3. Paste the girl with the bow in her hair two seats behind the driver.
4. Paste the boy wearing the cap in the front seat.
5. Paste the girl with the curly hair in the seat behind the boy wearing the cap.
6. Paste the angry boy in the back seat.
7. Draw yourself in an empty seat.
8. Draw a friend in the other empty seat.

Following directions
© 1990 by Incentive Publications, Inc., Nashville, TN.

Name _____

OUR FLAG

Color the flag.
Read the poem below.
Choose a rhyming word to write in each blank.
On the back of this page, write a poem about the flag.
(The poem does not have to rhyme!)

OUR FLAG

This is our flag
Of red, white and _____ ,
Its fifty stars
Shine clear and _____ .
We proudly watch
With heads held _____ ,
When our country's flag
Goes parading _____ .

Rhyming Words
few
high
fly
new
few
sky
blue
spry
true
by

Following directions/using rhyming words
© 1990 by Incentive Publications, Inc., Nashville, TN.

Name _____

SIGNAL WORDS

Many signs have pictures instead of words.
These signs are safety signals.
Do you know what they mean?

1. This means _____ .

2. This means _____ .

3. This means _____ .

4. This means _____ .

Draw a sign in this box that would
   be helpful to people.
Where would you put the sign?
Why?

*Answer Key

Understanding signal words
© 1990 by INCENTIVE PUBLICATIONS, Inc., Nashville, TN.

Name _____

It's for the birds!!!!!!!!!!

Everyone can think of several things
   they have to do that seem silly,
   dumb or _____ .
          (your word)

Write about three things you have to do that are really "for the birds"!

1. _____

   _____

   _____

2. _____

   _____

   _____

3. _____

   _____

   _____

What can you do to change these things?
Make suggestions on the back of this page.

Critical thinking
© 1990 by Incentive Publications, Inc., Nashville, TN.

Name _____

HORSING AROUND

Read each predicament and think about what is happening.
Write a sentence to describe how you would act if this really happened to you.

1. You are walking to the front of the room. Jim sticks out his foot and trips you. Everyone laughs.

   _____

   _____

2. You are walking to the lunch table carrying a bowl of soup. Dana throws a wadded up paper lunch sack at the trash can and it lands in your soup!

   _____

   _____

3. You are walking down the stairs. When you reach the bottom of the stairs, three kids you do not know race down the stairs and run into you, causing you to fall. They drop their books and shout at you. The principal walks over to see what is happening.

   _____

   _____

4. You walk into the restroom and find four students from your class writing on the wall.

   _____

   _____

Share your thoughts with one other person in the class.
How are your responses different?

Reasoning
© 1990 by Incentive Publications, Inc., Nashville, TN.

Name _____

what next?

Look at this picture story.
Write the letter of each picture box in the correct space below to show the order
    of the events.

First   _____
Second   _____
Third   _____

Draw your own picture story below.
Cut out the picture boxes and ask a friend to put them in the correct order.

Read the beginning of the story "Babbit The Circus Clown" to the class. Have the students suggest possible endings before completing the story.

BABBIT THE CIRCUS CLOWN

Babbit was a circus clown. His parents were in the circus, too. His father trained black bears and taught them wonderful tricks. The bears danced, tossed balls and jumped rope. Babbit's mother wore a special costume that sparkled like stardust when she flew through the air on the trapeze. Sometimes Babbit thought she looked like a beautiful butterfly fluttering through the air.

Once Babbit tried to help his father with the bears, but the big bears frightened Babbit. Then he thought that he would like to fly through the air like his mother, but he was afraid to climb the ladder. Babbit tried it once, but he came down very quickly. It was just too high.

One day Babbit heard some circus people talking about how wonderful his father was. Then they said that his mother was splendid on the trapeze. But they did not say one word about Babbit.

Babbit went to the animal cages and looked at the sleeping bears. Even when the bears were asleep they frightened him! He went into the big top and looked up at the high wire and trapeze. His heart beat faster. Babbit knew what he had to do.

(Stop here.)

16

Stop reading the story at this point and ask the students to think of endings for the story. You may do this in several ways:

1. Discuss the story orally and ask the students to suggest possible endings. Write each ending, as briefly as possible, on a chart or the chalkboard.

2. Have each student draw a picture of Babbit and write an original story ending.

3. Divide the class into small groups and ask each group to write an ending. Let each group share its ending with the class.

Note: Remember, there is no correct ending!

Now, read the story ending below. After completing the story, ask the class to choose the ending they like best and to explain their choice.

When Babbit returned to his room that night, he carefully planned what he would do for the next circus performance.

The next day, Babbit put on his favorite clown suit, the one with the purple and red stars and patches. He carefully put on his silly clown face and then looked at himself in the mirror for a long time. Then he made his smile even bigger! He was ready.

When Babbit walked into the center ring, the children laughed and clapped. Babbit knew that all he had to do was to be the best clown that he could be. He danced and did cartwheels. He popped a big balloon and fell on the ground. He walked over to a little girl and pretended to pick a flower from her ear. She hugged him and said, "You are the very best clown in the circus." Babbit smiled happily. He knew that he had made the best choice. He would always be Babbit the clown!

Play this "paper video game"!

There are six little frogs — three have freckles and three have stripes.

Each frog may jump over one, two or three mushrooms.

Two frogs can never be at the same place at the same time.

How can the striped frogs get to the left and the freckled frogs get to the right in only eight jumps?

Write the eight jumps on the lines below.

The first one has been done for you.

(Hint: You may want to use checkers or buttons to figure out how to do it!)

1. _____ # 2 jumps to # 1 _____

2. _____

3. _____

4. _____

5. _____

6. _____

7. _____

8. _____

When you have finished, ask your teacher for the correct answer.

Use the back of this page to make up your own "paper video game."

Ask a friend to play the game!

Problem solving/logical thinking
© 1990 by Incentive Publications, Inc., Nashville, TN.

*Answer Key

Name _____

My goals and activities for the week of _____.
(week)

Monday	Tuesday
Wednesday	Thursday
Friday	Next week I plan to: _____ _____ _____ _____ _____

Setting goals/making schedules
© 1990 by Incentive Publications, Inc., Nashville, TN.

Name _____

A DAY AT THE ZOO

Join Joe and Sara on a fun-filled journey through the zoo.

Read the sentences below and fill in the blanks.
Draw a path through the zoo to show the route that Joe and Sara took.

1. Joe and Sara entered the zoo and walked past the refreshments and giraffes to the _____ .

2. Then they continued straight and walked past the big cats to the _____ .

3. From there they walked to the next exhibit which was the _____ .

4. After looking at the colorful birds, they turned left to visit the_____ .

5. Then they turned left and passed the zebras to get to the _____ .

6. Joe and Sara laughed at the monkeys and then turned _____ to see the elephants.

7. After taking an exciting elephant ride, they discovered that they were lost. In what direction did they have to turn in order to exit the zoo? _____

On the back of this page, write about what you think Joe and Sara liked best about the zoo.

Following directions
© 1990 by Incentive Publications, Inc., Nashville, TN.

*Answer Key

REASONS FOR WRITING

To be an effective writer, one must have a mastery of basic skills and must have something to say. Yet, regardless of how well you "hone" the language skills of your students, a blank piece of paper often represents a closed door. Stimulation is the key that opens that door!

You must trigger the students' minds and pens in order to put their hands in motion. When students explore and understand the reasons for writing, their interest and performance improve.

The activities in this chapter are "invitations" to write. There are things for students to think about and decisions for students to make. You have taught the basic skills — now it's time to encourage your students to put those skills to good use!

CHAPTER 2

Name _____

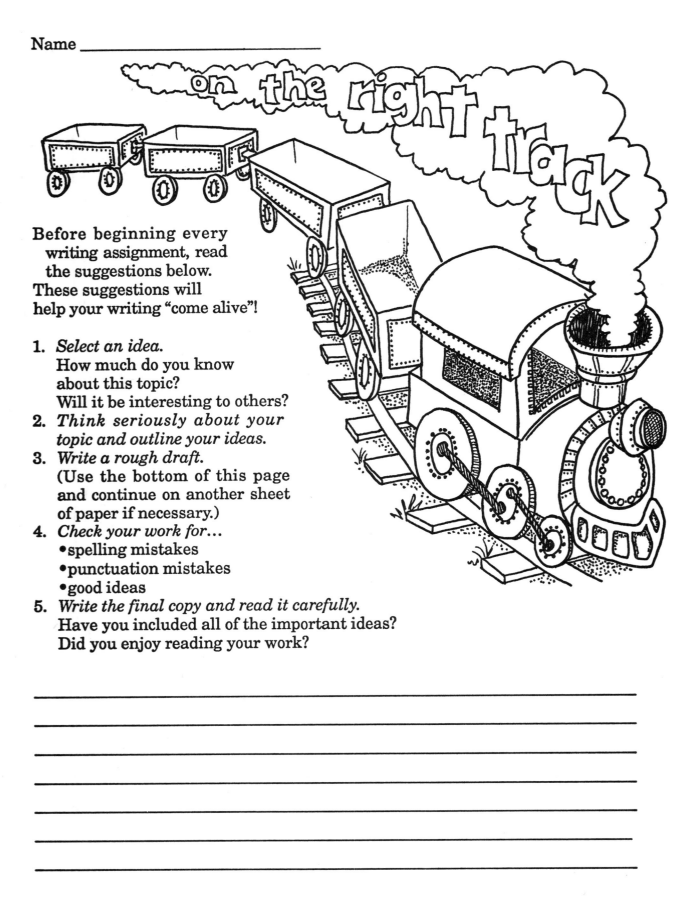

on the right track

Before beginning every
  writing assignment, read
  the suggestions below.
These suggestions will
  help your writing "come alive"!

1. *Select an idea.*
   How much do you know
   about this topic?
   Will it be interesting to others?
2. *Think seriously about your
   topic and outline your ideas.*
3. *Write a rough draft.*
   (Use the bottom of this page
   and continue on another sheet
   of paper if necessary.)
4. *Check your work for...*
   • spelling mistakes
   • punctuation mistakes
   • good ideas
5. *Write the final copy and read it carefully.*
   Have you included all of the important ideas?
   Did you enjoy reading your work?

_____

_____

_____

_____

_____

_____

_____

Learning process writing
© 1990 by Incentive Publications, Inc., Nashville, TN.

A CLASS YEARBOOK

Just For Teachers

Each week during the school year, select one student to write a "week in review" article. (Reproduce the form below.) The student can write about a current event or a class or school "happening." Collect the writings throughout the year and bind them together to make a class yearbook. Students will enjoy reading their yearbook of memories!

By _____

Date _____

_____

_____

_____

_____

_____

_____

_____

Picture/Illustration

Name _____

POETRY FOR TWO

TAKE TIME TO RHYME

Add your own rhyming words
to complete the sentences
below.

1. Mat the cat

   sat on a _____ .

2. Rin-tin-tin

   was very _____ .

3. See the flea

   jump on _____ .

Write a short rhyme about the
above picture.

_____

_____

_____

_____

HAIKU FOR YOU

A haiku is a poem with three lines of
five, seven and five syllables
respectively.

First line	5 syllables
Second line	7 syllables
Third line	5 syllables

Example:

Snow on the rooftops
Wild geese on the frozen pond
Today, winter came

Write a haiku below.

_____

_____

_____

Name _____

Read the ballooning words on this page.
Think of other ballooning words and write them in the spaces provided.
Write a "balloon" poem in this hot-air balloon.

**Ballooning
Words**

free
flying
high
rooftops
wind
sky
floating
air
treetops

**Other
Ballooning Words**

_____

_____

_____

_____

_____

_____

Writing poetry/visual imagery
© 1990 by Incentive Publications, Inc., Nashville, TN.

WRITE STUFF

A good way to stimulate reluctant writers is to focus on their interests and abilities. Here are two activities that do just that!

DEAR ME

1. At the beginning of the school year, have each student write a letter to himself or herself.
2. Urge the students to note any good times or problems they are having and to write about special events taking place at home or school.
3. Have the students put their letters in self-addressed envelopes and seal the envelopes.
4. Keep the letters in a safe place until the end of the school year.
5. At the end of the year, let the students open and reread their letters. Provide time for the students to discuss their reactions to their letters.

WHEN I GROW UP

1. Ask each student to think about three things that he or she can do well.
2. Have the students cut pictures "illustrating" their skills out of magazines and paste the pictures on sheets of construction paper.
3. Provide "thinking time."

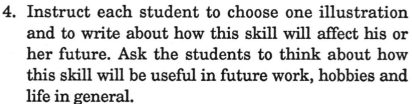

4. Instruct each student to choose one illustration and to write about how this skill will affect his or her future. Ask the students to think about how this skill will be useful in future work, hobbies and life in general.

Note: Some students will need your positive assistance in listing their attributes.

Name _____

proofreading ✓ list

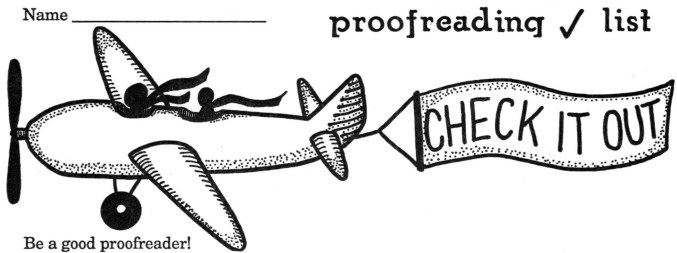

CHECK IT OUT

Be a good proofreader!
Use this proofreader's checklist whenever you write.

1. The first word in each sentence begins with a capital letter. _____
2. Each sentence ends with the correct punctuation mark. _____
3. All words are spelled correctly. _____
4. Each proper noun begins with a capital letter. _____
5. Each new paragraph is indented. _____

Editing Marks		
Mark	Use	Meaning
℮	The ~~the~~ time is now.	delete
∧	The th^ree kittens lost their mittens.	insert
≡	t̲r̲y it again.	capitalize
/	I'll S̸ee you later.	set in lower case
◯	(Their) going away.	check spelling

Write a short paragraph about a make-believe vacation.
Proofread the paragraph and use the editing marks explained above to correct
the paragraph.

_____

_____

_____

_____

Proofreading
© 1990 by Incentive Publications, Inc., Nashville, TN.

Name _____

in the beginning
story ender

At the bottom of this page is the ending of a story about a haunted house.
Write the beginning and middle of the story in the space below.
Give the story a title!

_____
(Title)

_____

_____

_____

_____

_____

_____

_____

_____

_____

_____

_____

The old house does not look
haunted anymore. The broken
windows have been replaced,
the roof has been repaired,
and it has a shiny new coat of
paint. Once again, the old
Johnson place looks grand.
It's "lived in" and loved!

Name _____

SARGE
STORY ENDER

At the bottom of this page is the ending of a story about a police dog named
   Sarge.

Write the beginning and middle of the story in the space below.

You may use any of the following "helping" words:

buddy, sheriff, child, robbery, wounded, hero

Be sure to give the story a title!

_____

(Title)

_____

_____

_____

_____

_____

_____

_____

_____

Sarge is not on the police force anymore. He has

been retired for several years. His shiny

medals hang on his doghouse. Sarge still

looks mean, but everyone knows that he

has a marshmallow heart!

WISE BIRD
word puzzles

Complete each word puzzle by writing the correct word beside each picture.

1. | | | s | h | |

2. | b | | a | |

3. | | | r | |

Write the words in the spaces below.

1. _____ 2. _____ 3. _____

Write a sentence using these three words.

_____.

Cut three pictures out of a magazine and paste them on the back of this page.
Make a word puzzle for each word.
Write one or two letter "clues" in each word puzzle.
Have a friend solve the puzzles!

Using picture clues
© 1990 by Incentive Publications, Inc., Nashville, TN.

Name _____

LENNIE

the helpful lightning bug

These sentences tell a story about
   Lennie.
Write the sentences on the lines
   below in the order you like best.

Before long, it started to get dark.

They saw an old lady drop her key.

Lennie went to see his friends.

They flew around together and had fun.

1. _____

2. _____

3. _____

4. _____

Write a sentence to end the story.

_____

_____

Sequencing/determining sentence order
© 1990 by Incentive Publications, Inc., Nashville, TN.

Name _____

my Delightful, Descriptive Paragraph

1. Look at the picture on this page. Write several words that describe the picture.

   _____

_____

2. Plan a descriptive paragraph about the picture. What is the main idea?

   _____

3. What are some details you will include in the paragraph? _____

   _____

4. Write your paragraph in the space below.
   Remember to begin the paragraph with the main idea.
   Indent the first word of the paragraph.

   _____

   _____

   _____

   _____

Now, proofread your descriptive paragraph.

Writing descriptive paragraphs
© 1990 by Incentive Publications, Inc., Nashville, TN.

Name _____

where on earth would you go?

Think about a country that you would like to visit.
Complete the sentences below.

1. If I could visit any country in the world, I would choose _____ .

2. I could write to _____ to ask for more information
   about this country.

3. I would like to know more about _____
   _____
   _____ .

4. This country interests me because _____
   _____
   _____ .

Writing about chosen topics

Name _____

WELCOME TO THE NEW SCHOOL YEAR!

Write a letter to your teacher telling how you feel about school and what you would like to do this year.

Dear _____ :

_____

_____

_____

_____

_____

_____

_____

Sincerely,

_____

hats off to you!

Congratulations, _____,

for _____!

Your teacher is congratulating you for something you do well!
In the space below, draw a picture and write a brief paragraph to "show and tell"
    what you do well!

Recognizing skills & accomplishments

Name _____

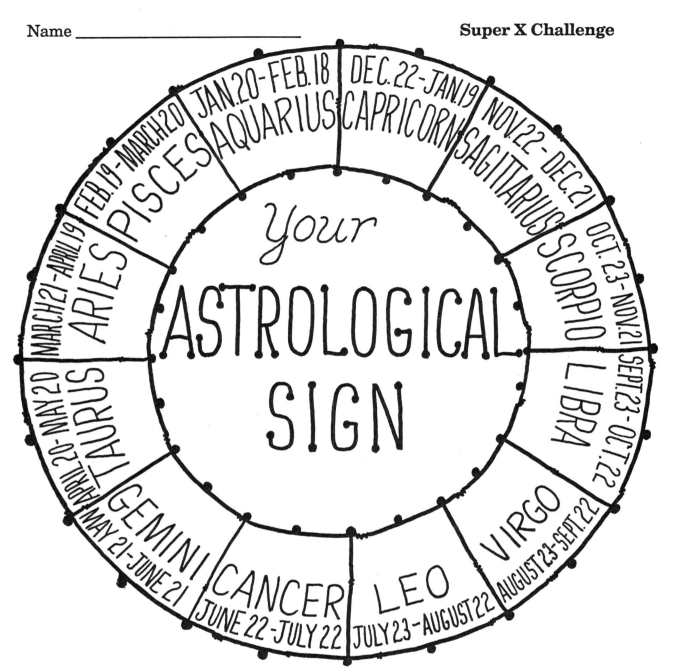

Find your birthday on the chart to determine your astrological sign.
Write your sign below.

I am a _____ .

Go to the library and find out as much as you can about your astrological sign.
Read your daily horoscope in the newspaper.
Compare the "predictions" with what really happens during the day on the back
   of this page.
Was your horoscope accurate?
Write a few sentences on the back of this page to tell what you think about your
   horoscope.

Using research skills/writing
© 1990 by Incentive Publications, Inc., Nashville, TN.

CHAPTER 3

STIMULATION FOR READING

Students who like to read enjoy exploring new dimensions and look forward to the opportunity to read. Students who do not enjoy reading or who need help in developing reading skills require more "reading incentive." This chapter contains the success-oriented (high-interest/low-vocabulary) activities you need to provide that incentive.

Most of the materials in this chapter do not require students to give "correct answers" and can be easily adapted for various reading levels. You may need to give individual help to reluctant readers and/or use the activities in small support groups.

Regardless of the level on which the class is functioning, your students will thrive on the stimulation that you provide!

is for AUTHOR

Introducing students to the concept of authorship is the first step in helping them "to know" the creators of their favorite books.

Write a simple definition of the word author on poster board and display it in a prominent place in the classroom.

Example: An author is someone who writes a story, poem or play.
Many authors write stories about themselves.

Try these activities!

KNOW AN AUTHOR
Feature one author each month. Gather as many books as you can that this author has written. Read several selections to the class and encourage the students to read other selections on their own. Display book jackets and illustrations from the books.

WRITE AN AUTHOR
After the students have been exposed to several authors, let the class choose a favorite author. Write a "class letter" to the author on chart paper, or have each student write a letter and illustrate a scene from a favorite story the author has written. (You may want to write a letter asking the author for an autographed picture or book. The teacher's involvement often gets results!) Send all of the letters to the author in one large envelope!

BECOME AN AUTHOR
Have the students write their own stories. Feature one story each week on a bulletin board having the caption "Our Own Author Of The Week."

going **BATS** over Halloween

Help decorate the classroom for Halloween with black bats!
These step-by-step directions are easy to follow if you
read them slowly and carefully.
Before you begin, look at the illustrations.
Note that there is a letter in each corner of the diagram.
Refer to the illustrations as you complete each step.

1. Fold a six-inch square of black construction paper in half diagonally. Press the crease firmly.
2. Unfold the paper.
3. Fold the paper in half diagonally in the opposite direction.
4. Unfold the paper. Notice how the fold lines "cross" at the center (point E).
5. Pinch the paper at point E, pushing the triangles AEC and BED inward as you flatten triangles CED and AEB.
6. Fold point D toward the center so that there is a vertical line from point E to point D.
7. Fold point C toward the center so that there is a vertical line from point E to point C. (Lines EC and ED should meet in the center of triangle AEB.)
8. Fold point E forward half an inch to make the bat's head.
9. For an "eerie" effect, cut "curves" in the wings.
10. Hang the bat from points A and B.

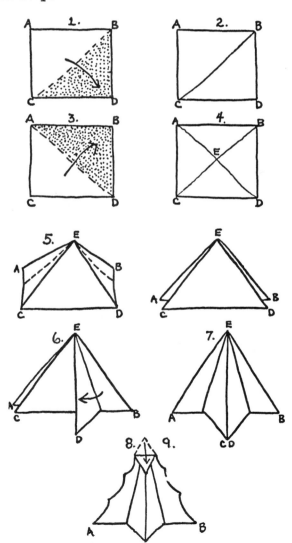

Reading & Following directions
© 1990 by Incentive Publications, Inc., Nashville, TN.

THREE KIDS AND A DOG

Read this story
Then answer the questions on page 41.

THREE KIDS AND A DOG

"What a vacation!" said Mr. Bird. "I've been packing this car for hours. It's not easy going on a trip with three kids."

"Now, dear, we'll have fun," said Mrs. Bird. "The children will help to make it extra special."

"Sure, Dad," cried all three kids from the back seat, "it will be great!"

"Move over, Jerry, you are taking up too much space!" shouted Katie.

"Quiet, dear," said Mother. "Your father has a headache. Let's stop and eat now, Fred. I think all of us are hungry. Besides, we could use some exercise!"

The Bird family enjoyed a picnic lunch of tuna sandwiches and fruit. They took a short walk in the woods and then began to pack their things.

"Where did Susie go?" asked Mr. Bird. "She knows better than to wander off like that."

The family began looking for Susie. They searched the rest area and then went into the nearby woods. Suddenly, they heard a dog barking. They followed the sound and found Susie crying under a tree.

"I hurt my foot and this nice doggie found me. Look, Daddy, he has no collar and he is very dirty. I know he has no home," Susie said.

"What a vacation," said Mr. Bird as they began driving down the highway again. He winked in the mirror at the children.

"Oh well, what's a vacation without three kids!" he said.

"Three kids and a dog," Susie said happily.

Reading comprehension
© 1990 by Incentive Publications, Inc., Nashville, TN.

WHAT DID YOU READ?

1. How many Birds were in the car? _____

2. Was Mr. Bird upset at the beginning of the story? _____

   Why? _____

3. Do you think the children were having fun at the beginning of the story?

   Why? _____

   _____

4. What did they eat for lunch? _____

5. How did they find Susie? _____

   _____

6. Why did Mr. Bird wink at the children? _____

   _____

WHAT DO YOU THINK?

7. Should Susie's parents have been angry with her? _____

8. What do you think about the Birds taking the dog with them?_____

   _____

9. What should they do with the dog? _____

   _____

10. Do you like to go on vacations with your family? _____

    Why? _____

Reading comprehension
© 1990 by Incentive Publications, Inc., Nashville, TN.

*Answer Key

Name _____

THIS BOOK

Complete this book report to tell about a book you have read.

Book Title _____

Author _____

I thought this book was _____

Helping words: good, fine, story, interesting, characters.

Look in the book for more words that will help you!

Writing simple book reports

Name _____

REAL or

Read each story below and
decide whether it is real or
make-believe.
Circle the correct answer.

1. **The Golf Ball** A man hit a golf ball high into the air. A bird flew by, caught the ball in its beak, and took the ball home to show its family. real make-believe	**2.** **A Cold Day** It was a cold winter day. Rick went outside to play, but he didn't have fun because it was just too cold. Even his snowman looked cold! real make-believe
3. **The Race** Amy was a good runner, and her friend Emily was a good runner, too. Amy ran the best that she could, but Emily won the race. Amy smiled at her friend and gave her a hug. real make-believe	**4.** **Alligator Soup** Tammy had an alligator friend named Sam. One day Tammy invited Sam to eat lunch with her. "What are you having for lunch?" Sam asked. "Alligator soup," Tammy replied. "No thanks," said Sam, "I can't have lunch with you today." real make-believe

Find a real book and a make-believe book in the classroom or library.
Write the titles below.
Choose one book to read.

*Answer Key

Real book: _____

Make-believe book: _____

Distinguishing between real & make-believe
© 1990 by Incentive Publications, Inc., Nashville, TN.

STELLAR SPELLER

This fun game for six players will add pizazz to any spelling class!

Preparation
- Use 3" x 5" index cards to make a set of 25 spelling cards. Write a spelling word on each card.
- Reproduce the game sheet (page 45).

How To Play
1. Provide your "stellar spellers" with a set of 25 word cards.
2. Select one person to be the "reader."
3. Have each of the other five players select a star point (A, B, C, D, or E).
4. Ask the reader to pronounce one spelling word for player A.
5. Player A spells the word. Then the reader checks the spelling against the word card.
6. If player A spells the word correctly, he or she keeps the word card and writes the word on the game sheet (in section A).
7. If player A misspells the word, the reader pronounces the word for player B.
8. Play continues in this manner until the word is spelled correctly.
9. Continue this process for all five star points.
10. The winner is the first person to fill his or her section of the game board with correctly spelled words.

Options
1. Have a student prepare the word cards. This saves you time and provides the student with spelling practice.
2. Use an overhead projector to enlarge the game board. Use markers and oak tag to make a large floor game. Laminate the game board or cover it with Contact paper. Have the students use erasable markers when playing the game.
3. Have the students play the game as a relay race. Provide each "row" of students with a game board and a separate set of word cards.
4. This game is a good remediation device for slow learners! (You act as the reader.)

Name _____

Read and follow the directions below.

1. Draw a face in the circle.
2. Write your name beside the square.
3. Draw a picture of a house in the rectangle.
4. Draw a door and two windows on the house.
5. Draw a dog in the square.
6. Draw a tree next to the house.
7. Draw a red collar on the dog.
8. Draw a chimney on the house.
9. Color the triangle yellow.
10. Make a black X in the triangle.

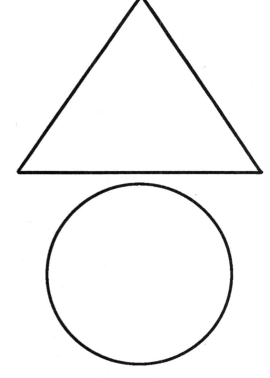

Reading & following directions

Name _____

mother goose lost

Some of the words of this Mother Goose rhyme are missing.
Can you find them?

1. Read the rhyme.
2. Find the missing words in the picture.
3. Write the words in the blanks.

Humpty Dumpty _____ on a wall.

Humpty Dumpty had a _____ fall.

All the king's _____

And all the _____ men,

Couldn't _____ Humpty Dumpty

Together again.

Finding missing words
© 1990 by Incentive Publications, Inc., Nashville, TN.

MOTIVATING
THE
RELUCTANT READER

These success-oriented activities will help reluctant readers develop healthy attitudes toward reading!

PARTNERS READ

Having students share stories with classmates helps to make reading fun. Let the students work in pairs. Assign a simple story to each pair. Instruct each student to read either the first or second half of the story and to "tell" that part of the story to his or her partner. Each pair of students will become familiar with the "whole" story but will do only half the reading!

STUMPERS

Choose a favorite "simple" book. Select sentences from the book and write them "out of sequence" on a sheet of paper. List the numbers of the pages on which the sentences may be found, but do not "match" the sentences with the page numbers. Have a student read the pages listed and then write the sentences in the correct order.

Just For Teachers

TEASERS

- Cut short articles out of magazines. Ask the students specific questions that can be answered only after the students have read the articles.

- Gather resources containing information about various sports and hobbies. Make simple reading cards that require students to look up information in the resources. Record "instructions" for the students on a cassette tape and place the tape, a tape recorder and the resources in a reading center for the students' free-time use.

UPSIDE-DOWN READING

Choose a simple poem that has only a few words in each line. Read the poem to a student and then ask the student to read the poem silently. Turn the poem "upside down" and have the student read it aloud!

EDIBLE READABLES

Have the students bring empty food boxes to class (cereal boxes, snack boxes, etc.). Scan the labels or "reading matter" on the boxes and make up questions about the information. Record the questions on tape, write them on paper, or ask them orally. The tentative reader will enjoy perusing the boxes to find the answers! Encourage the students to involve family members in this kind of activity at home. Reading at the breakfast table can become a habit!

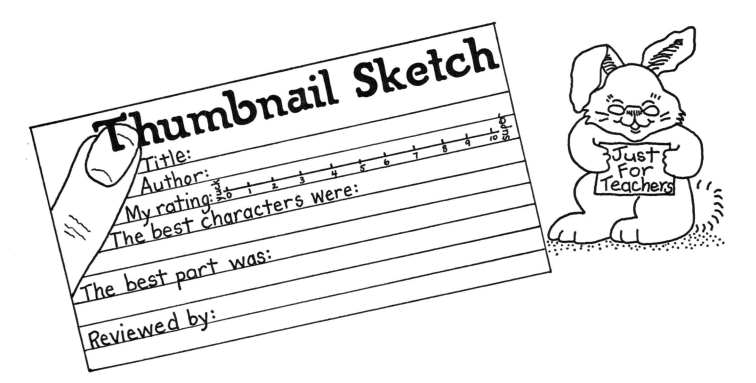

Thumbnail Sketch

Title:
Author:
My rating: just so-so 0 1 2 3 4 5 6 7 8 9 10 super
The best characters were:

The best part was:

Reviewed by:

Just For Teachers

A book report card file is a handy classroom resource! This "thumbnail sketch" file is a great way to stimulate student interest and help students make book selections.

1. You will need a card file box and 3" x 5" index cards.
2. Prepare a sample card (such as the one shown above) for the students' reference.
3. Divide the file box into sections with "category" cards. Choose categories according to the interests of the class and add new categories throughout the year.
4. Write "rules" for using the file and for checking the accuracy of the information. Tape the rules to the inside of the file box as shown.
5. Instruct the students to write a "thumbnail sketch" card for each new book they read.

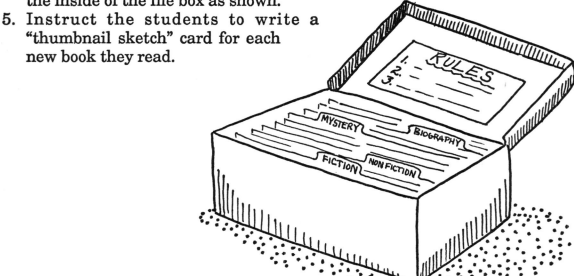

Name _____

Complete the "magic carpet" book report below.

Title: _____

Author: _____ Number of pages: _____

Main characters: _____

_____

Summary (in your own words): _____

_____

_____

_____

_____

Ending: _____

_____

_____

Would you recommend this book to a friend? _____

What did you like about the book? _____

_____

_____

Type of book (check one):

Adventure ____   Mystery ____   Biography ____   Nonfiction ____   Other ____

Writing a book report
© 1990 by Incentive Publications, Inc., Nashville, TN.

BOOKMARK AWARDS

Reproduce these bookmark awards and give them to
students when appropriate. The students can color the
bookmarks and glue them to oak tag "backings."

YOU ARE A
WINNER

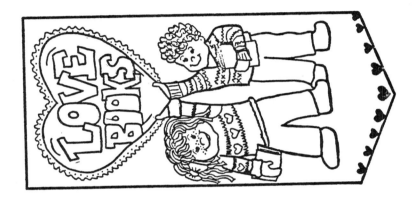

LOVE BOOKS

READING...
the KEY to FUN
and LEARNING

READERS ARE
KINGASAURUSES

CLUES FOR COMPUTATION

Most teachers have tons of manuals, textbooks and curriculum guides for teaching math. What teachers need and want are creative "reinforcing" activities for student practice. This chapter provides you with a wide range of stimulating activities with high-interest, contemporary themes and graphics to help you successfully extend and reinforce basic math skills.

Several "blank" work sheets with attractive illustrations are included to enable you to create activities that are appropriate for your class. Your remedial, average and above-average students will benefit from your "personal touch"!

Name _____

NOT TOO LATE

LOOK AT THE CLOCK

WHAT TIME IS IT ?

_____

Refer to the clock above to answer these questions:

1. What time will it be 2 $\frac{1}{2}$ hours from the time shown? _____
2. You ate lunch 25 minutes ago. What time did you eat? _____
3. Dinner will be served in 5 hours and 20 minutes. What time will it be then?
   _____
4. What do you think will happen approximately 9 hours from the time shown?
   _____
5. What time was it 3 hours and 25 minutes earlier than the time shown?
   _____
6. Set these clocks:

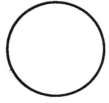 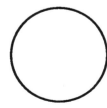 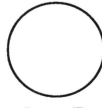 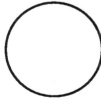

Wake Up Time   Bedtime   Leave For School Time   Dinner Time

Telling time

*Answer Key

Bunny Money

The Bunny family is counting their coins so they can go to the Tree Stump General Store to buy more carrots.

How much does each member of the Bunny family have?

1. Susie has: = $ _____

2. Timmy has: = $ _____

3. Mama Bunny has: = $ _____

4. Papa Bunny has: = $ _____

5. Grampa has: = $ _____

6. How much do they have all together? = $ _____

Adding coin values

© 1990 by Incentive Publications, Inc., Nashville, TN.

*Answer Key

Name _____

Cut out the cupcake "tops" below.

Match each numeral with the correct number word and paste the cupcake tops
   in place.

Color numerals 2, 7 and 10 pink.

Color numerals 3, 4 and 8 brown.

Color the other numerals any color you choose.

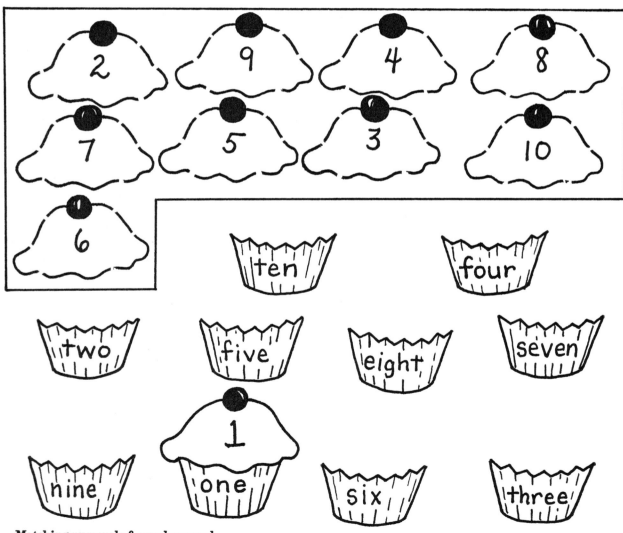

Matching numerals & number words

Name _____

Work each math problem below.
Then use the code to "decode" the secret message.

9 −5	6 +2	8 −7

6 −3	5 +4	8 −2

7 −5	4 +3	1 +2	7 +2	9 −4

Write the message here:

_____

Use the code to write a message to a friend!

CODE	
1	U
2	S
3	A
4	Y
5	T
6	E
7	M
8	O
9	R

Working addition/subtraction problems
© 1990 by Incentive Publications, Inc., Nashville, TN.

*Answer Key

Name _____

Work the math problems
below.

HALLOWEEN
problems

WOOOoo...

COMPUTER

Help the computer complete this magic square.
The numbers in every row must add up to 15 (horizontally, vertically and diagonally).

Hint: Try writing the numbers 1–9, one at a time, in each box.

	5	

Now that you've checked your answer and know how to work a magic square, make your own magic square for a friend to solve!
It's harder than it seems!

*Answer Key

Solving magic squares/number puzzles
© 1990 by Incentive Publications, Inc, Nashville, TN.

TOPSY TURVY MATH FACTS

This self-correcting manipulative activity is a great way to reinforce math skills!

Materials:
    wooden ice cream spoons
    index cards
    box or Manila envelope

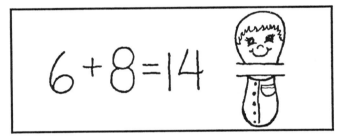

Procedure:
1. Have the students use markers to turn wooden ice cream spoons into people!
2. Write math problems (of the appropriate skill level) on index cards. Write some problems with correct answers and some with incorrect answers.
3. On the back of each card, draw a "smiling" face if the answer is correct or a "frowning face" if the answer is incorrect.
4. Cut two slits in each card as shown to make a "slot" for a "spoon person."
5. Place the cards and "spoon people" in a box or Manila envelope.
6. Write simple student directions on the box (see those below) and place the activity on a work table or in a learning center. Have the students complete the activity individually or in pairs during their free time.

Student Directions
1. Read a math problem.
2. If the answer is correct, insert a "spoon person" in the card slot "head up." If the answer is incorrect, insert the "spoon person" in the slot "head down."
3. Turn the card over to check yourself. If you see a smiling face, the answer on the card is correct. If you see a frowning face, the answer on the card is incorrect.

Name _____

HOLIDAY PROBLEMS

Addition and subtraction problems are hidden horizontally and vertically.
Circle as many problems as you can find and add the symbols +, − and = where needed.
One has been done for you.

4	5	3	9	5 + 5 = 10	3
6	1	7	4	3	8	4	2
2	5	6	11	4	9	3	1
7	6	4	5	3	8	2	9
6	3	7	2	9	10	1	3
4	2	6	3	7	3	3	6
5	9	3	6	4	10	7	8
1	4	3	4	7	6	5	10

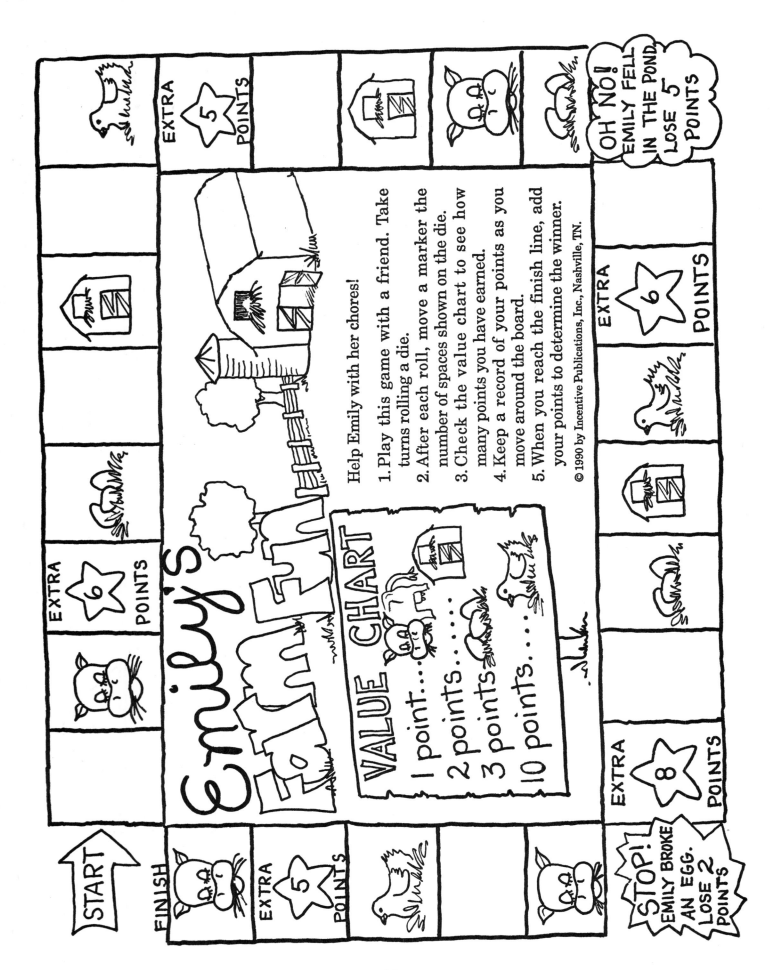

Help Emily with her chores!

1. Play this game with a friend. Take turns rolling a die.
2. After each roll, move a marker the number of spaces shown on the die.
3. Check the value chart to see how many points you have earned.
4. Keep a record of your points as you move around the board.
5. When you reach the finish line, add your points to determine the winner.

© 1990 by Incentive Publications, Inc, Nashville, TN.

VALUE CHART

1 point.....
2 points.....
3 points.....
10 points.....

EXTRA 5 POINTS

EXTRA 6 POINTS

EXTRA 6 POINTS

EXTRA 8 POINTS

EXTRA 5 POINTS

OH NO! EMILY FELL IN THE POND. LOSE 5 POINTS

STOP! EMILY BROKE AN EGG. LOSE 2 POINTS

START

FINISH

62

Work the math problems below.

Valentine problems

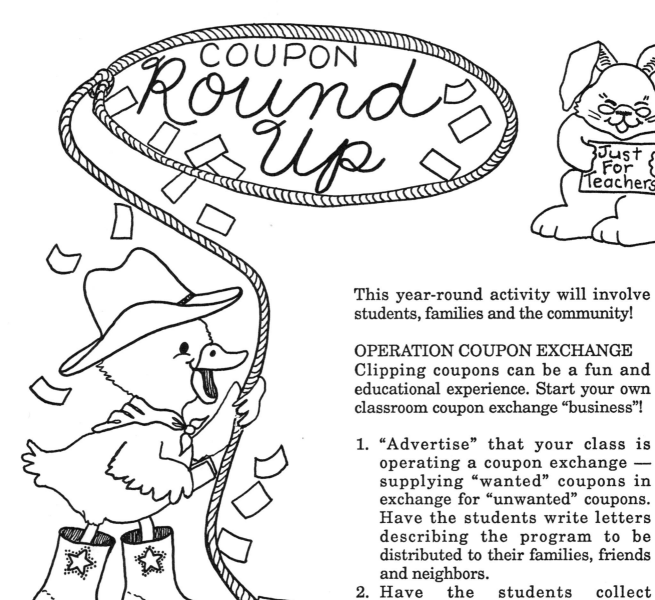

COUPON Round Up

This year-round activity will involve students, families and the community!

OPERATION COUPON EXCHANGE
Clipping coupons can be a fun and educational experience. Start your own classroom coupon exchange "business"!

1. "Advertise" that your class is operating a coupon exchange — supplying "wanted" coupons in exchange for "unwanted" coupons. Have the students write letters describing the program to be distributed to their families, friends and neighbors.
2. Have the students collect "unwanted" coupons from their families, friends and neighbors and exchange them for "requested" coupons from the class file. Have the students file the collected coupons in a large box according to specific categories.
3. Ask each student to keep a log of money saved by his or her family (or friend, neighbor, etc.) as a result of using coupons. Have the students collect their grocery "register tapes" to verify their logs.
4. At the end of the project, give a small prize to the student whose family saved the most money!

OTTO'S AUTO MAZE

START

6	12	5	48	54	60	66	72
3	18	4	42	36	30	7	78
53	24	30	20	33	24	8	6
65	7	36	15	12	18	26	12
74	48	42	19	6	47	30	18
60	54	8	72	78	17	30	24
66	59	9	66	60	54	36	42
72	78	6	7	53	48	43	48
63	74	12	21	36	42	60	54
19	19	18	24	30	26	66	FINISH

Take Otto through the auto maze.
Begin at start and draw a line through the maze by connecting the multiples of
  six—in order!
You may move vertically or horizontally, but not diagonally.
When you reach 78, move to the nearest six and start again!

Recognizing multiples of six/multiplication
© 1990 by Incentive Publications, Inc., Nashville, TN.

*Answer Key

Name _____

DRAGON MATH

Work the math problems below.

WOW! THESE ARE TOUGH, BUT YOU CAN DO IT!

Name _____   **Super X Challenge**

APPLE AL'S ORCHARD

TODAY
MACINTOSH $3.00 bushel
GOLDEN DELICIOUS $2.00 ½ bushel
GRANNIE SMITH $.50 pound
WINESAP $.30 peck

4 pecks = 1 bushel

Help Apple Al fill apple orders!
Compute the totals for the orders below.

Total

1. Mr. Benson ordered a bushel of Winesap apples. $_____

2. Mrs. Jones wants one bushel of Golden Delicious apples. $_____

3. Your teacher ordered two bushels of Macintosh apples and
    one bushel of Golden Delicious apples. $_____

4. T. Kent wants ten pounds of Granny Smith apples, but he
    is returning a peck of Winesap apples for credit. $_____

5. Mr. Bundt wants two bushels of the cheapest apples. $_____

6. Buy one peck of your favorite apples. $_____

7. What is the total for today's orders? $_____

Using math operations
© 1990 by Incentive Publications, Inc., Nashville, TN.   *Answer Key

Name _____

THE SUPER DELUXE, PLEASE!
What a sandwich!!

Check a newspaper or grocery store ad to find the prices of the items below.
Write the prices in the blanks.

HAM
$ ___ lb.

TURKEY
$ ___ lb.

SALAMI
$ ___ lb.

★ TODAY'S DELI SPECIALS ★
Bologna $___ lb. American cheese $___ lb.
Roast Beef $___ lb. Swiss cheese $___ lb.

How much will this super deluxe sandwich cost to make?

3 slices of ham (18 slices per pound) $ _____
2 slices of turkey (16 slices per pound) $ _____
4 slices of salami (20 slices per pound) $ _____
2 slices of bologna (18 slices per pound) $ _____
2 slices of roast beef (8 slices per pound) $ _____
1 slice of swiss cheese (20 slices
     per pound) $ _____
2 slices of American cheese (16 slices
     per pound) $ _____

                        Total cost: $ _____

These people have special orders.
Figure the costs of their sandwiches.

Amy does not want cheese. $ _____
Emily wants twice as much ham and
     no turkey or salami. $ _____
Eric wants twice as much cheese and $ _____
     no salami.

Solving addition/subtraction/multiplication/division problems
© 1990 by Incentive Publications, Inc., Nashville, TN.

Name _____

Work the math problems below.

Name _____

CHEF'S CORNER

Calling all cooks!
Cooking involves math skills when it is
 necessary to adjust ingredient
 amounts in recipes.
Adjust the penuche candy recipe as
 instructed below.

Penuche Candy
2 cups brown sugar
2/3 cup milk
3 tablespoons butter
1 cup chopped nuts
½ teaspoon vanilla

1. You want to triple the recipe.
    Write the recipe below.

2. You want to make one-fourth the
    recipe.
    Write the recipe below.

Here's how to make penuche candy:
1. Mix sugar, milk and butter in a
    saucepan.
2. Cook slowly for 15 minutes.
3. Remove from heat.
4. Add nuts and vanilla and beat
    until creamy.
5. Pour into shallow, buttered pan
    to cool.
6. When cool, cut into squares.

Understanding fractional parts
© 1990 by Incentive Publications, Inc., Nashville, TN.

*Answer Key

70

Name _____

Work
the math
problems on
this page.

BRAIN "QUIZLER"

Work these problems on the back of this page.

1. How would you write 16 fours (4s) so that their sum equals 1,000?

    (Hint: 44 + 44 = 88)

2. A man is digging a thirty-foot pipeline. He digs three feet an hour and then rests one hour. How many hours will it take him to dig the pipeline?

3. Seventeen toothpicks are arranged to make six boxes.
    • Remove six toothpicks so that two boxes are left.
    • Remove five toothpicks from the original figure so that three boxes are left.

4. A woman counted her change and found that she had 100 coins which totaled $5.00. What coins did she have?

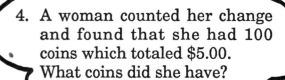

*Answer Key

Solving math problems
© 1990 by Incentive Publications, Inc., Nashville, TN.

CHAPTER 5

PROMOTING HEALTH AND SAFETY

Today's fast-moving world requires that increased attention be given to physical and mental health. In the elementary grades, students are forming habits and establishing lifestyle patterns. These are the very complex, formative years. What an important role the teacher has!

Nineteen pages dealing with important health topics are included in this chapter. A few activities address the more serious health and safety issues. Each activity presents a brief introduction of a health topic and requires the students to think and react. It is intended that the activities will encourage positive responses.

Choose the activities that fit into your curriculum and are appropriate for your students. Be sure to incorporate follow-up discussion and other related activities to reinforce the concepts learned.

Name _____

STRANGERS GOOD and BAD

There are both good and bad strangers.
Do you know the difference?

Ask an adult to help you read the sentences below.
Then fill in the blanks.
Talk about your answers together.

1. Jay moved to a new town. He did not have any friends yet. He sat on the steps and watched the other kids play. He is a _____ stranger.

2. A man in a car stops and asks you if you would like a ride home. He is a _____ stranger.

3. You are lost in a store. A police officer asks you if you need help. He is a _____ stranger.

4. A woman you do not know is standing outside the playground fence. She offers you some candy. She is a _____ stranger.

5. One of your mom's new friends comes to your house for dinner. You've never seen her before. She is a _____ stranger.

6. Dad left you alone in the car for a few minutes while he went into the bank. A man knocked on the window and asked to talk to you. He is a _____ stranger.

Learning about good & bad strangers

Name _____

HEALTH HELPERS

These are health helpers.
They help to keep us well.
Read the sentences and fill in the blanks.
Color the picture.

DOCTOR   NURSE   OPTOMETRIST

1. A _____ examines me and tells me what medicine to take.

2. An _____ gives me an eye test.

3. A _____ takes my temperature when I do not feel well.

4. The _____ tells me if I need glasses.

5. If I fell and hurt myself, the _____ would give me stitches.

6. The school _____ calls my parents when I am sick.

7. My doctor helps me because _____.

8. The school nurse helps me when_____

_____.

9. The optometrist can help me if _____

_____.

Name _____

Trisha's tonsils

Tonsils are small organs located at the back of the mouth on each side of the throat.

Tonsils help us by "catching" the germs that get into our bodies we when breathe.

Sometimes tonsils become infected and a doctor must remove them.

Do you know someone who has had his or her tonsils removed?

Read the story below.
Then draw a picture in the empty window of Trisha after her operation.

TRISHA'S TONSILS

Trisha had a problem. She always had a sore throat and she had to stay inside when it was cold. She was very lonely when her friends were outside playing.

One day, the doctor told Trisha that it was time to take out the trouble makers — her tonsils. Trisha was worried because she thought that it would hurt.

Trisha was very glad that she did not have to stay in the hospital. She came home the same day she had the operation. Her throat was a little sore, but she was used to that.

In just a few days Trisha was feeling great. Now she could play outside with the other children — even in the snow!

On the back of this page, write three things that everyone can do to stay healthy.

Understanding health problems
© 1990 by Incentive Publications, Inc., Nashville, TN.

Name _____

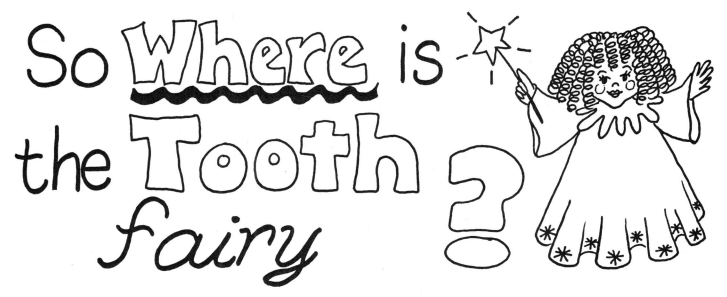

So Where is the Tooth fairy?

Teeth are very important.
They help you to chew and to speak clearly.
Most boys and girls lose their baby teeth between the ages of six and twelve.

Look into a mirror to see which baby teeth you have lost.
Make an X on each tooth that you have lost (on the picture on this page).
What is the correct "name" of each tooth?
Show your diagram to someone at home to be sure that you have marked the
     correct teeth.

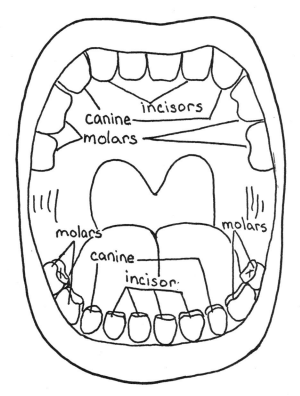

Write five important rules for proper
teeth care.

1. _____
   _____
2. _____
   _____
3. _____
   _____
4. _____
   _____
5. _____
   _____

my weekly exercise log

Keep an exercise log for one week.

Some activities to choose from include walking, running, biking, jumping rope, skating, swimming, and participating in physical games and sports.

	Exercise	Where	Time Spent
Monday			
Tuesday			
Wednesday			
Thursday			
Friday			
Saturday			
Sunday			

My plan to improve:

_____   _____

My signature   Parent's signature

Create an eye-opening bulletin board that features good ways to "start the day."

Construction:

1. Ask the students to bring the empty packages of their favorite healthy breakfast foods to class.
2. Have the students turn their food packages into simple train cars by adding construction paper wheels.
3. Ask several children to work together to make an engine for the train (cover a box with black construction paper).
4. Draw train tracks on the board or make tracks using strips of construction paper.
5. Attach the train cars to the board (connect them with strips of black construction paper) and add cotton "smoke."
6. Add the caption "Have A Better Breakfast Week — Give Your Train Go Power."
7. Write other healthy breakfast food suggestions on cards and attach them to the board.

Lead a discussion about nutritious breakfast foods. Have the students keep weekly logs of the things they eat for breakfast. Store the logs in a pocket attached to the board.

Suggestion: You may want to send a note to parents asking for their cooperation. Let the students plan a breakfast to honor their parents. Hold the breakfast in the classroom early one morning!

Name _____

Did you know that the food you eat affects how you feel?

If you skip breakfast, you might be low on energy at school.

If you eat "quick energy" foods for lunch (cookies, candy, ice cream, etc.), you might "slow down" in the afternoon.

Food does many good things for the body such as...
- keep it warm
- repair and build cells
- supply energy
- build strong muscles
- build strong teeth and bones

Go to the library and do some research to find out how specific foods help the body to function.

Use the information you gather to complete the chart below.

Food	What It Does For The Body

Do some more research to find out what foods are good choices and what foods are poor choices.

Use the information you gather to complete the charts on the next page.

Learning about nutrition/making wise food choices

Good Food Choice	Reason	Poor Food Choice	Reason

Good Things I've Eaten This Week	Bad Things I've Eaten This Week

Write a "good food plan" for the future on the back of this page.

Learning about nutrition/making wise food choices
© 1990 by Incentive Publications, Inc., Nashville, TN.

Name _____

Bicycle Safety Check

It's important to observe safety precautions when participating in any sport or exercise.

Part of bicycle safety is making sure your bike is working properly.

Make a bicycle safety check on your bicycle. If you don't have a bicycle, help a friend!

Part	OK	Things That Need To Be Done
Brakes		
Chain Tension		
Handlebar Grips		
Tire Pressure		
Tire Treads		
Seat Height		
Light		
Horn		
Reflectors		
Pump/Tools		
Other:		
Other:		

Why is it important to be a "safe bicyclist"?

_____

_____

Understanding bicycle safety
© 1990 by Incentive Publications, Inc., Nashville, TN.

Name _____

One evening Teddi was taking a long time to get ready for bed.
Her parents scolded her for wasting time.
Teddi felt sad because she thought her parents did not like her anymore.
What do you think?

Sometimes things happen that make you mad or sad.
When this happens, it often helps to talk about how you feel.

Check the right box to show how each "situation" would make you feel.

What About When . . .	Mad	Sad	OK
1. You are watching T.V. and someone changes the channel without asking you.	☐	☐	☐
2. You drop something and break it.	☐	☐	☐
3. You have a new baby brother or sister.	☐	☐	☐
4. Someone borrows your bike without your permission.	☐	☐	☐
5. You want to stay up late, but your parents say no.	☐	☐	☐
6. You do not like anything you are having for dinner.	☐	☐	☐
7. You can't go out to play because it's raining.	☐	☐	☐

Understanding feelings

Name _____

Every individual is special in some way.
Interview ten classmates to find out what makes them special and unique.
Then complete the chart below.

Name	Hobby	Likes	Dislikes
1.			
2.			
3.			
4.			
5.			
6.			
7.			
8.			
9.			
10.			

What interesting things did you discover? _____

_____

_____

_____

Appreciating individual differences
© 1990 by Incentive Publications, Inc., Nashville, TN.

Name _____

LITTERBUG WALK

Litter is a type of pollution that everyone can help to control.
You can help by picking up litter everywhere you go.

Your teacher will take your class on a litter walk.
Take a large sack with you and collect as much litter as you can.
After the walk, empty your litter sack and write the number of each "kind" of litter you collected on the chart below.

Work with three friends to complete this outline.

FOUND LITTER	✓
BOTTLES	
CANS	
PAPER	
BOXES	
GARBAGE	
OTHER	

<u>What We Can Do To Control Litter</u>

A. Our Families
   1. _____
   2. _____
B. Our Class
   1. _____
   2. _____
C. Our School
   1. _____
   2. _____
D. Our Community
   1. _____
   2. _____
E. The Media
   1. _____
   2. _____

On the back of this page, write your plan for controlling litter.
Select one part of the plan that you can carry through and "take action"!

Expressing environmental concerns
© 1990 by Incentive Publications, Inc., Nashville, TN.

Name _____

ALL-STAR
SAFETY STUDENT

Grade yourself from 1 (low) to 10 (high) on your safety performance this week.
Total your points.
How did you score?

1–10

1. I looked both ways whenever I crossed the street.

2. I wore my seat belt whenever I rode in a car.

3. I did not run at school.

4. I chewed my food carefully whenever I ate.

5. I did not play rough at recess.

6. I was quiet during the last fire drill.

7. I did not put foreign objects in my mouth.

8. I did not talk to strangers.

9. I did not run up or down stairs.

10. Other: _____

My total score: _____

Score Chart
1–5   Try to do better next week!
6–7   Keep trying! You're almost an "all-star safety student"!
8–12   Fantastic! Keep up the good work!

Recognizing safety precautions
© 1990 by Incentive Publications, Inc., Nashville, TN.

86

Name _____

MAGIC WORDS

BY PROFESSOR HARE

Certain words and phrases can "work magic" such as *please* and *thank you*.
Professor Hare is here to help you learn some other magic words!

1. The most important six words are:
   "I admit that I was wrong."

2. The most important five words are:
   "You did a great job."

3. The most important four words are:
   "You must be proud."

4. The most important three words are:
   "I am sorry."

5. The most important two words are:
   "Thank You."

6. The least important word is "I."

List other "magic words."
1. _____
2. _____
3. _____
4. _____
5. _____
6. _____

How do these words "work magic"?
Why do you think the word *I* is least important?
Write a plan for using magic words today!

_____

_____

_____

_____

_____

Name _____

THE ENEMY

Many kids today are overweight because they eat too much
  junk food and don't get enough exercise.
Respond to the statements below by checking either yes or no.

		Yes	No
1.	I always eat a healthy breakfast.	_____	_____
2.	I avoid junk food at lunch.	_____	_____
3.	I exercise after lunch.	_____	_____
4.	I do not watch too much television.	_____	_____
5.	I exercise on weekends.	_____	_____
6.	I eat fruit every day.	_____	_____

		Yes	No
7.	I get enough sleep (at least eight hours).	_____	_____
8.	I know about the four food groups.	_____	_____
9.	I drink at least five to six glasses of water a day.	_____	_____
10.	I eat/drink three or more cups of milk or milk products each day.	_____	_____
11.	I eat only healthy snacks.	_____	_____
	Total:	_____	_____

Score Chart

Yes Answers	Your Score
9-10	You're terrific!
7-8	Not bad!
6 and below	Watch out for "the enemy"!

Check the "score chart" to see if you need to watch out for "the enemy" — junk
  food!
If your score is 6 or below, what can you do to improve your eating and exercising
  habits?

_____

_____

Learning about good eating/exercising habits
© 1990 by Incentive Publications, Inc., Nashville, TN.

Name _____

CLONNING AROUND
CAN BE FUN

Clowning around or acting silly is OK when playing games or having fun on the playground, but it is not OK when eating in the school cafeteria or crossing the street.

Make a check beside each line below to tell if you think clowning around is OK or not OK in that situation.

	OK	Not OK
1. When riding the school bus	____	____
2. When working in the classroom	____	____
3. When playing at home	____	____
4. When visiting a *very* sick friend	____	____
5. When having fun at a birthday party	____	____
6. When shopping in the store	____	____
7. When eating in a restaurant	____	____
8. When playing in your backyard	____	____
9. When swimming in a public pool	____	____
10. When walking in the hallway at school	____	____
11. When entertaining guests at home	____	____
12. When playing at a friend's house	____	____

Complete this sentence:

I like to clown around when _____

_____

Learning about acceptable behavior
© 1990 by Incentive Publications, Inc., Nashville, TN.

Construct this self-concept bulletin board and use it as a vehicle for enhancing the self-image of every student in your class!

Construction:
1. Cover the board with brightly colored paper.
2. Draw two children (a boy and girl, with their arms above their heads as shown) on butcher paper or construction paper. Cut out the figures, add features with markers and attach them to the board.
3. Write the caption "Tell Us What You Do Well" on two construction paper signs (see above) and attach the signs to the children's hands as shown.
4. Draw a "talk balloon" pattern (as seen in comic strips) on white paper and make a copy for each student.
5. Ask each student to think about what he or she does well. (You might want to give personal examples.)
6. Ask each student to write a statement about himself or herself on scrap paper and to rewrite it on the talk balloon. (Write examples of correct punctuation on the chalkboard if necessary.)
7. Let the students staple their talk balloons on the board. Allow time for a class discussion about "feeling good about yourself."

Options:
- Have the students work in small groups. Instruct each student to make a talk balloon for someone else in the group.
- You may need to help slow or shy students determine what they can do well.

A HEALTHY ME
FROM A to Z

Play this game with one or more friends to see who knows the most "healthy habits"!

1. Place your markers at start.
2. The first player rolls a die and moves that number of spaces. The player then must name a good "health habit" that begins with the letter in that space. (Example: "A" — Always brush after meals.)
3. If the player is able to name a good health habit, he or she may stay on that space and wait for his or her next turn. If not, the player must go back to where he or she was.
4. The game continues in this manner until someone reaches the finish line and becomes the winner!

START

FINISH

A D G K O S W B E H L P T

Z B M S G N D O

MOVE AHEAD 3

C J W R P D E K

B C F I J M Q V A N R U Y

MOVE AHEAD 2

Name _____

HAVE A SAFE HALLOWEEN

Find and circle the Halloween safety words in the word puzzle.
Then write about how you will have a safe Halloween on the pumpkin below.

B	L	A	N	T	E	R	N	K
F	G	X	P	A	R	E	N	T
C	A	R	E	F	U	L	Z	M
D	N	O	F	M	A	S	K	T
S	R	C	O	S	T	U	M	E
S	A	F	E	T	R	E	A	T

Understanding Halloween safety/finding hidden words
© 1990 by INCENTIVE PUBLICATIONS, Inc., Nashville, TN.

92   *Answer Key

CHAPTER 6

INSPIRATION FOR FUN AND GAMES

Who says that school can't be fun? A "spirited" classroom helps to make learning "come alive"! All you need to create this excitement in your room is a little inspiration.

Most everyone can remember at least one outstanding teacher from his or her childhood — one that added "sparkle" to the dreariest of days. She or he no doubt had a well-worn "bag of tricks" — special ways of reaching out to the "unreachable" or challenging capable students. Learning was satisfying in such a classroom!

The ideas and activities in this chapter are relatively simple to prepare and present. Most of the needed materials are easily accessible. Some materials are even self-contained within the activity. Within this chapter you'll find games to play, skills to reinforce, and "seasonal fun" — all with interesting formats. ...*You* be the one they remember!

Mind Your ABC's

Add these three fun alphabet games to your list of "winners"!

All of your students will enjoy this active, alphabetizing relay race!

1. Make two "decks" of word cards by writing one spelling or vocabulary word on each card.
2. Set up a game area in which two teams (comprising the entire class) may stand or sit in two rows.
3. Place a table between the two rows (at the front) and place the two card decks on the table (the cards in each deck should not be in alphabetical order). Take the top three cards from each deck and place them on the table (removing the rest of the cards from the table).
4. Instruct the first student in each team row to run to the table, to alphabetize a stack of word cards, and to run to the back of his or her team row.
5. Check each stack of cards to be sure they have been alphabetized correctly. If the cards have been alphabetized correctly, remove them and place a new stack of three cards in their place. If the cards have not been alphabetized correctly, place them on the table for the next student.
6. Play continues in this manner until one team has correctly alphabetized its entire deck of cards.

Because some students will be more capable than others, let these students form teams to play this "B" version of the alphabet game. Follow the same rules as above, but have each student alphabetize the entire deck of cards (placing the cards in one long row). Play continues until all of the members of one team have correctly alphabetized the deck of cards. (This "B" version will take longer to play!)

Can you remember the favorite alphabet game "Aunt Abigail Went On A Trip"? Have the students take turns adding to an alphabetical listing of things to pack in a suitcase for a trip.

> Example: "Aunt Abigail went on a trip and packed an alarm clock, a baseball cap, a coat, etc."

If you wish, have the students name items belonging to a specific "theme" — a circus, zoo, etc.

Just For Teachers

94

Most students are fascinated by television, movie and sports "stars." Capitalize on this interest by involving the students in this creative thinking activity!

1. Cut pictures of popular "stars" out of magazines and newspapers and mount them on construction paper.
2. Draw a large star pattern and cut lots of stars out of sturdy paper. Write a "topic" related to "stars" on each star shape.
3. Ask each student to choose a celebrity from the collection of pictures and to pick a star shape at random.
4. Instruct the students to write short paragraphs or stories as directed by the topics on their star shapes.

Note: This activity can be used as a "verbal game" if desired.

BUDDIES, PALS and Friends

Here's a super icebreaker for the beginning of a new school year!

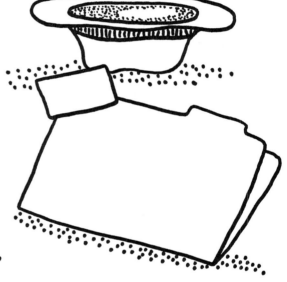

Materials Needed:
- Manila folders (one for each student)
- 3" x 5" index cards (one for each student)
- box or hat
- copies of page 97 (one for each student)

Directions:
1. Give each student a Manila folder. Ask the students to label their folders "Buddies, Pals And Friends."
2. Ask each student to write his or her name on a 3" x 5" index card. Place the cards in a box or hat.
3. Let half the class draw one card from the box. If a student draws his or her own name, ask the student to draw another card. (Return all of the cards to the box.)
4. Instruct each student to interview the classmate whose name he or she drew by using the interview form on page 97. Remind the students to draw pictures of their new friends!
5. Repeat this procedure daily until each student has interviewed at least half the class.

Just For Teachers

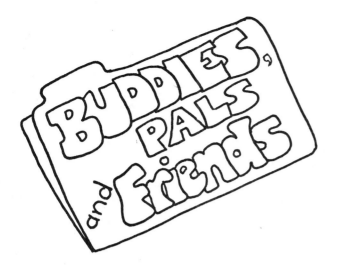

Interview a new friend!
Complete this interview form as
    your friend answers the questions.

My name _____

Classmate's name _____

Address _____

Brothers & Sisters (names & ages) _____

_____

Pets _____

What is your favorite school subject? _____

What do you like to do after school?

_____

Do you have a hobby or favorite sport?

_____

What are your favorite T.V. programs?

_____

Draw a picture of your new friend in the box above.

Conducting an interview

TIME FOR RE-LEAF

Gather an assortment of fall leaves and press them in a phone book overnight. The next day, try one or more of these "re-leaf" activities with your class.

Give each student a leaf. Tell the students that they have two minutes to find others who have the same kind of leaf. Once the students have formed "leaf groups," instruct each group to write a poem about fall. Encourage expression through the use of the five senses!

Use the above procedure for having the students form groups. Then instruct each group to use their leaves and a few art supplies to create "animals." Have each group write a story about the animal and its environment and habits.

Give each "leaf group" an index card on which an imaginary situation has been written. For example: "You are a leaf and have just been blown into a pile of leaves." Have each group dramatize the situation for the rest of the class.

Let the students create oversized leaves to hang from the ceiling. Instruct the students to tear autumn colors of tissue paper into pieces and to overlap the pieces on waxed paper. Have the students glue the tissue paper in place by brushing liquid starch over the paper. When the starch dries, the students may cut their papers into leaf shapes!

Just For Teachers

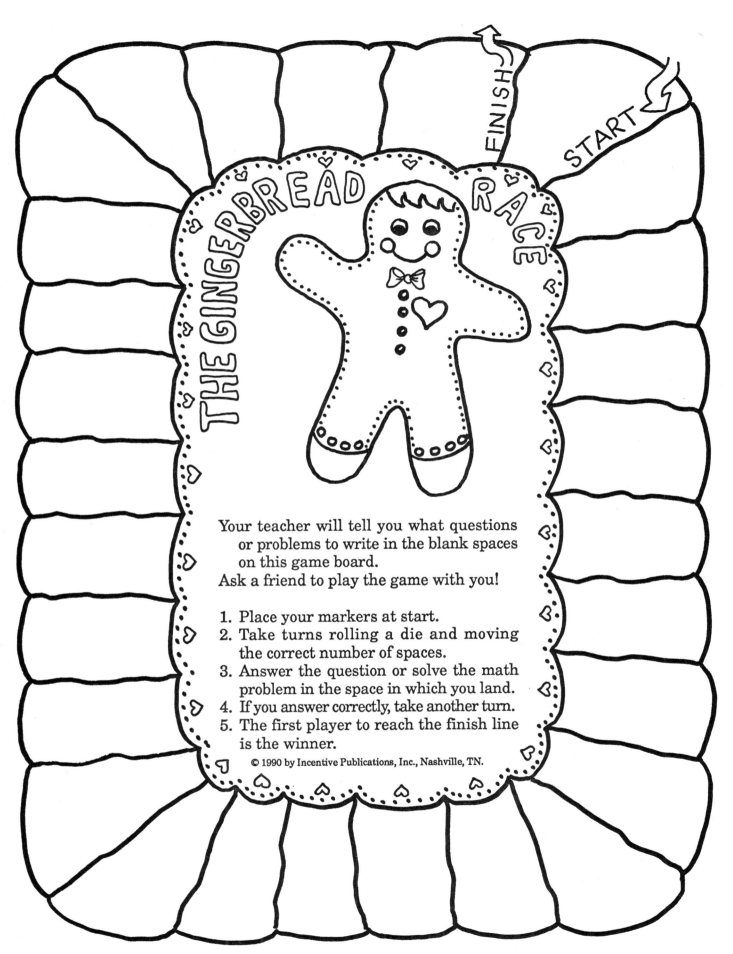

FINISH

START

THE GINGERBREAD RACE

Your teacher will tell you what questions or problems to write in the blank spaces on this game board.

Ask a friend to play the game with you!

1. Place your markers at start.
2. Take turns rolling a die and moving the correct number of spaces.
3. Answer the question or solve the math problem in the space in which you land.
4. If you answer correctly, take another turn.
5. The first player to reach the finish line is the winner.

THE SLEEPY GIANT

Students of all ages will love this vigorous outdoor game which combines listening skills with locomotor activity.

How To Play:
1. Draw or "mark" two lines approximately thirty feet apart.
2. Have the students stand side by side on one of the lines.
3. Choose one student to be "the sleepy giant" and have the student lie down in the center of the area between the two lines.
4. Instruct the giant to call out "Here comes Sleepy Giant" and to jump up and run towards the other students.
5. This is the signal for the students to run from one line to the safety of the other line. The object is not to be tagged by the giant.
6. As the students are tagged by the giant, they must remain in the center with the giant. The game continues until all of the players have been tagged.
7. The giant can play tricks by calling out "Here comes Peter Rabbit" or some other name. If a student runs after hearing anything but the correct words, he or she must join the giant in the center.

Variations:
- Have the players hop or skip between lines.
- Have the giant name certain colors. Only the players wearing those colors may run.
- Have the giant call out months. Only players whose birthdays fall in those months may run.

SEASONAL OUTREACH

Reproduce these ready-to-use seasonal patterns and use them for classroom decorations, bulletin board decorations, additions to student work sheets, etc. (The patterns may be enlarged on an overhead projector.)

Just For Teachers

I LOVE YOU

Students will enjoy playing this simple playground game. When working with very young children, repeat the directions several times and demonstrate the game for the children.

How To Play:

1. Have the students form a circle. Choose one student to be "it" and have that student stand in the center of the circle.
2. Instruct the player who is "it" to throw the ball into the air as he or she calls out the name of a classmate.
3. The classmate named runs into the center of the circle and tries to catch the ball. If he or she succeeds, that student becomes "it."
4. Play continues in this manner for the desired length of time. (Encourage the children to call the names of those who have not been called.)

Variations:

- Have the student who is "it" call out "to the right of Jim" or "to the left of Liz" (substituting names of classmates) to indicate who is to try to catch the ball.
- Write each student's name in large letters on poster board. Have the student who is "it" to hold up name cards rather than calling out names.
- Have the student who is "it" to call out articles of clothing rather than names to indicate particular students (example: red ribbon and red socks).

102

Here's a fun way to write without using a pencil!

Directions:
1. Collect magazines, newspapers, brochures, junk mail, and other types of "printed material."
2. Divide the class into small groups.
3. Provide the group members with scissors, a box and written materials to be "cut."
4. Instruct the students to cut out individual words they especially like. (The size, shape and print type should vary.)
5. Have the students in each group place their chosen words in a box.
6. Give each group a large piece of paper and instruct them to paste their words on the paper to write a creative story, newspaper article or letter (see theme list below).
7. Display the finished products for all to read and enjoy!

Possible Themes

- Hot Dogs & Peanut Butter
- The Singing Easter Bunny
- Cross County Caper
- Hazel The Witch
- Go-Cart Gala
- Snowman Lives!

- Puppy Love
- Galloping Bumblebees
- Leaping Lizards
- Dear Santa...
- Queen's Delight
- Gus The Grouch

Preparation:
- Stress to the class that it is good to feel proud of a job well done. Identify students that have excelled in some way. Be sure to include non-academic areas!
- Ask each student to bring a snapshot of himself or herself to class.

Construction:
1. Cover the board with colorful construction paper.
2. Cut the caption "Join The Proud Crowd! You Are Great" out of construction paper and attach it to the board.
3. Attach construction paper "cutouts" of the children to the board, or take a group photo of the class and attach it to the board.
4. Make a "Hall of Fame" poster on which to write the names of the weekly "winners" and attach it to the board.
5. Leave space on the board to attach the weekly winner's photo, proud crowd application and other pertinent "information" and "materials."

Procedure:
1. Each week, provide the students with proud crowd applications (see below). The students may fill out the applications at school or take the applications home for parent input.
2. Explain that each student is to write about a job well done or one in which he or she has improved. It may be school work, a home activity, a sport, a helpful act, etc.
3. Select a weekly "winner" and keep it a secret! Collect the materials to display on the board, including the winner's photo, and prepare the display for the following week. Students will enjoy walking into the classroom to see whose face is on the board!

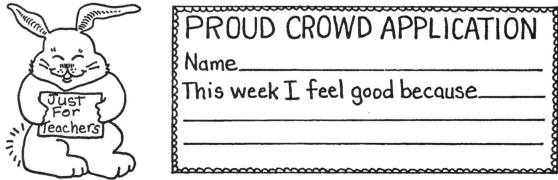

© 1990 by Incentive Publications, Inc., Nashville, TN.

PUDDLE JUMPIN' rainy day Nonsense

When the weather's wet and full of gloom,
Try some laughs to warm your room!

Write each of the following riddles on an index card. Let the students take turns reading the riddles to classmates. Be sure to write the answers on the backs of the cards.

1. What animal jumps higher than a house? (None — a house can't jump.)
2. Why do humming birds hum? (They don't know the words.)
3. Why are elephants so wrinkled? (They are too big to iron.)
4. What fish can you put on your breakfast table? (Jelly fish.)
5. What is the best thing to put into apple pie? (A fork.)
6. What has three feet but doesn't wear shoes? (A yardstick.)

Just For Teachers

7. What room has no windows or doors? (A mushroom.)
8. What bird is most like a car? (A goose, because it honks.)
9. Why do soldiers always sleep late on April 1? (They just finished a March of 31 days.)
10. What is Smokey the Bear's middle name? (the)

Dear _____ ,

Please come to a _____ !

What: _____

When: _____

Where: _____

Held by: _____

Please join us for

_____ !

Time: _____   Place: _____

Your friends _____

PARENT SUMMER PLAN

Summer vacation sometimes can be a drag, even for the most creative parents and children. When the routine of school ends, many youngsters still need direction and purpose for those endless summer days. Responsibility as a teacher ends when the students walk out the door on the last day of school. However, your interest and influence can extend well into the summer months!

The following parent plan gives suggestions for 24 fun-filled days. Some activities can be directed from "afar," whereas others need active parent participation.

Possibilities For Implementation

1. Write a suggestion sheet to be attached to the parent plan. Send the papers home with the students.
2. Hold a parent meeting to discuss the ideas on the parent plan sheet. Encourage the parents to contribute their own suggestions and solutions for summer enrichment. Make a list of the ideas on the chalkboard for the parents to copy.
3. Ask the students to help write a class letter which explains the activity sheet. The letter may be copied, attached to the parent plan, and sent home with each student.

Points To Stress

1. In most cases, activities need not follow a sequence.
2. Remind parents that excitement can be generated by discussing plans for the activity well in advance.
3. Ask the students to look over the suggestions and to select their favorites.
4. Be sure that the needed materials are readily available.
5. Parent involvement will help make each activity special. The inclusion of a friend can make an activity extra special!

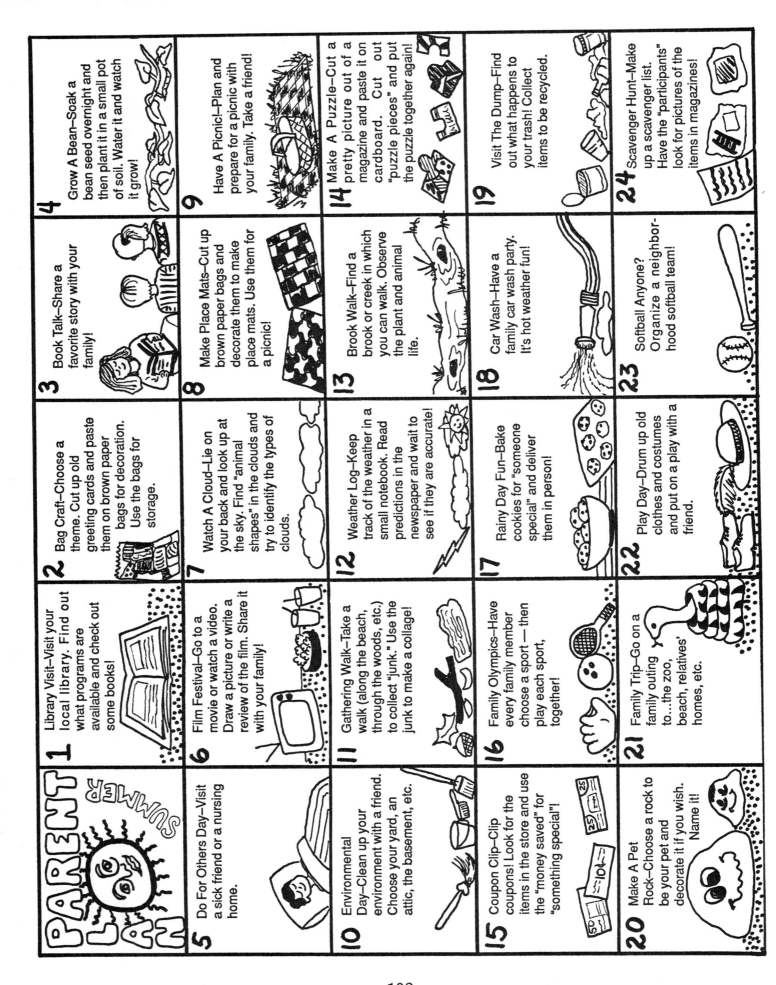

PARENT A LAN SUMMER

1 Library Visit–Visit your local library. Find out what programs are available and check out some books!

2 Bag Craft–Choose a theme. Cut up old greeting cards and paste them on brown paper bags for decoration. Use the bags for storage.

3 Book Talk–Share a favorite story with your family!

4 Grow A Bean–Soak a bean seed overnight and then plant it in a small pot of soil. Water it and watch it grow!

5 Do For Others Day–Visit a sick friend or a nursing home.

6 Film Festival–Go to a movie or watch a video. Draw a picture or write a review of the film. Share it with your family!

7 Watch A Cloud–Lie on your back and look up at the sky. Find "animal shapes" in the clouds and try to identify the types of clouds.

8 Make Place Mats–Cut up brown paper bags and decorate them to make place mats. Use them for a picnic!

9 Have A Picnic!–Plan and prepare for a picnic with your family. Take a friend!

10 Environmental Day–Clean up your environment with a friend. Choose your yard, an attic, the basement, etc.

11 Gathering Walk–Take a walk (along the beach, through the woods, etc.) to collect "junk." Use the junk to make a collage!

12 Weather Log–Keep track of the weather in a small notebook. Read predictions in the newspaper and wait to see if they are accurate!

13 Brook Walk–Find a brook or creek in which you can walk. Observe the plant and animal life.

14 Make A Puzzle–Cut a pretty picture out of a magazine and paste it on cardboard. Cut out "puzzle pieces" and put the puzzle together again!

15 Coupon Clip–Clip coupons! Look for the items in the store and use the "money saved" for "something special"!

16 Family Olympics–Have every family member choose a sport — then play each sport, together!

17 Rainy Day Fun–Bake cookies for "someone special" and deliver them in person!

18 Car Wash–Have a family car wash party. It's hot weather fun!

19 Visit The Dump–Find out what happens to your trash! Collect items to be recycled.

20 Make A Pet Rock–Choose a rock to be your pet and decorate it if you wish. Name it!

21 Family Trip–Go on a family outing to...the zoo, beach, relatives' homes, etc.

22 Play Day–Drum up old clothes and costumes and put on a play with a friend.

23 Softball Anyone? Organize a neighbor-hood softball team!

24 Scavenger Hunt–Make up a scavenger list. Have the "participants" look for pictures of the items in magazines!

108

CHAPTER 7

TIPS FOR CREATIVITY

How can you harness creativity? Search for a unique twist — a new and different way of teaching or reinforcing the same old lessons. Your students will respond with enthusiasm, and that can be contagious!

Build on students' successes by touting them daily in unusual ways. You'll find that even slow learners will "blossom" when their accomplishments are acknowledged.

In this final chapter, you'll find imaginative ideas to supplement your creativity in the classroom and to extend it into the home. Good communication is the key to family involvement. Don't let your "sparkle" diminish when the school day has ended. Keep all lines of communication open. Parents can be an untapped resource — put it to use!

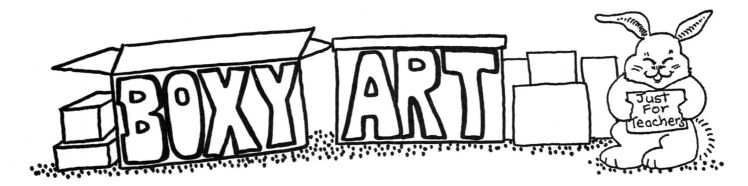

BOXY ART

To start "Boxy Art Projects" in your classroom, you'll need boxes of all shapes and sizes. Construction paper, glue, paint, markers and lots of "junk" will add the finishing touches. Be sure to give the students plenty of planning time before beginning each project!

- Turn a box upside down. Cut out an opening for a puppet stage. Stand the box "between" two desks (see illustration) and wrap large sheets of butcher paper around the desks to create a "hiding place" for the puppeteers.

- Have the students work in construction teams to create vehicles by "combining" boxes of various sizes. Juice cans can be used for wheels!

- Have the students create robots or space creatures by attaching "found junk" and other features to boxes. These make great motivators for stories or poems!

- Have the class work together to make a city of boxes. Strategically place the "buildings" on a large "class-made" map of a town — your town!

Note: Many exciting writing, social studies and math lessons can evolve from these box projects!

DICTIONARY MOBILES

Ask each student to look in the dictionary for a word beginning with the same letter as his or her name. The word should describe the individual in some way. Instruct each student to write his or her name, the "chosen" word and a brief definition on various shapes (see illustration). The students may punch holes in the shapes and string them together in "mobile fashion."

Follow the same procedure for the students' last names. Have them write the information on the "backs" of their mobiles. Suspend the mobiles from the classroom ceiling!

Extension:
Have the students copy all of the words and definitions to make personal dictionaries. The students can use their dictionaries to write stories!

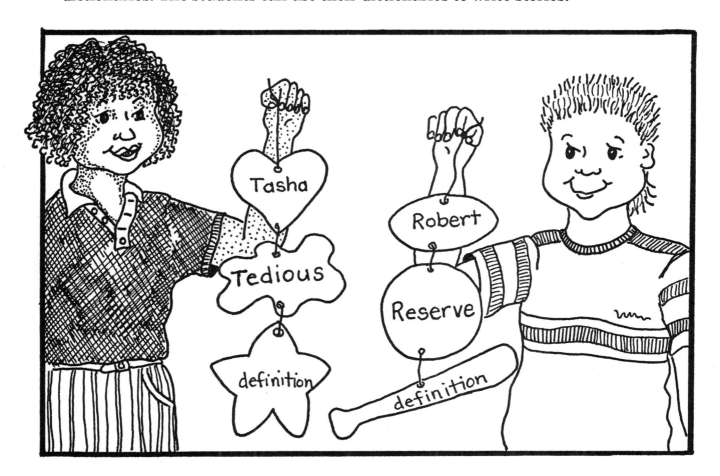

SEASONAL SCOOP

ATTENTION ALL STUDENTS!

Create a seasonal announcement board in your classroom. Make a life-size drawing and mount it on heavy cardboard. Fasten a clipboard to the drawing. Change your theme with the seasons! The announcement board is great for daily schedules, time changes or special notices.

Note: This idea also can be used as a bulletin board theme.

PICTURE MONEY DUE TUESDAY

Just For Teachers

ASSEMBLY TODAY 1:30 in the auditorium

Don't Forget! FIELD TRIP PERMISSION SLIPS

LOOK of the month club

Kids will feel ten feet tall when their work is displayed in this very important book!

Directions:
1. Reproduce this page and cut out the illustration at the top of the page. Color it with markers.
2. Tape or paste the illustration on the front of a photo album (the kind with clear plastic, self-sticking pages).
3. Let the students select their own "best work" to display in the class album.
4. The book may be continually changed and updated by inserting new work.

Be sure that every student has work in the class album. Keep the book "on display" so that students, parents and visitors may browse through the book.

MONKEY CAPERS

Trace this pattern onto cardboard and cut out a "supply" of monkeys. Hang oak tag monkeys around the classroom. Hook the monkeys together or hang them on a clothesline. Use the monkeys for "monkey capers"!

<u>Monkey Caper Ideas</u>

Write the following on monkey patterns…

- alphabet letters
- numerals
- math facts
- sight words
- student names
- classroom rules
- awards

PHOTO FINISH

Ask each student to bring old photographs to class — baby pictures and other "childhood" pictures — for class activities.

Baby Who? Send a note home with each student asking for a baby picture of the student. Ask the students to bring their baby pictures to class in sealed envelopes. Display the baby pictures on the bulletin board and number each picture. Ask the students to guess who the "babies" are!

Photo News Display pictures of the students on a bulletin board. Ask each student to select a picture and to write a newspaper story about the picture. Remind the students to include a date, headline and good "lead" sentence in their stories.

Photo Finish Bulletin Board Mount a picture of each student on a piece of construction paper, number each picture and display them on a bulletin board. Use the board in a variety of ways...

• Select several numbers and have the students write captions or titles for the pictures.
• Select one number and ask the students to write a poem or story about the picture.
• Select a number and have the students write letters to this individual.
• Think of other creative ideas!

Name _____

Shapely Art

Alice the artist has painted a picture.
Oh no, it fell and broke into pieces!
Help Alice put the painting together again.
Cut out the pieces below and paste them in the frame.
Then, color the painting!

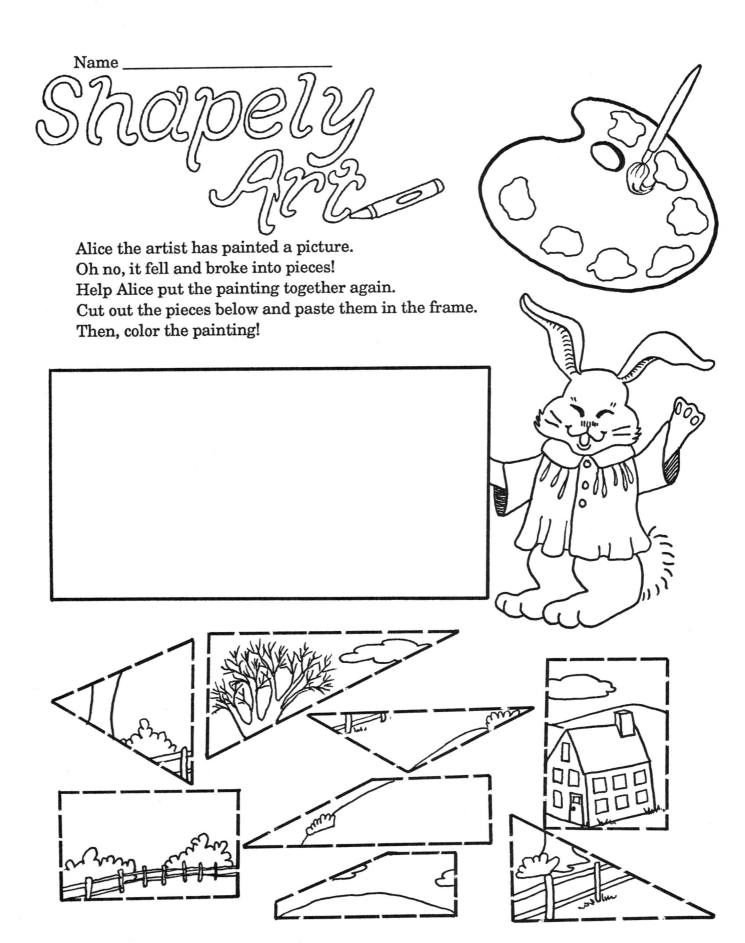

"BELONGING"

Just For Teachers

Bulletin boards make a big difference in every classroom — especially at the beginning of the school year. Choose one of the back-to-school bulletin boards below and "put it up" to start the year off right!

OUR MACHINE WON'T WORK WITHOUT YOU. GLAD YOU ARE HERE!

Keith · Trish · Barbara · Sean · Sonja · Alicia · Lavelle · Theresa · Tim · Lisa · Tom · Sue · Brian

SPECIAL DELIVERY A BIG **HELLO** TO MY NEW RESIDENTS. *Sincerely, Miss Smith*

Cheryl · Ryan · Bobby · Lana · Amy · Jenny · Evan · Angie · Dale · Leslie · Beth · John · Gina · Robbie · Ty

WELCOME THE TO BUNCH

Steve · Sara · Robbie · John · Andy · Sam · Leslie · Tim · Lydia · Luis · Tracy · Bob · Kim · Lynne · Pam · Kareem · Amy · Eric · Tim · Joe · Todd · Chris · Mark · Katy

FAMILIES AT HOME

There are certain things that everyone
can do to improve family relationships.
Number the statements below in their order of
importance, 1–5.
How important do you think each statement is?

Talk about your day at mealtime.   _____

Help with household chores.   _____

Discuss quarrels and how they can be avoided in the future.   _____

Talk about your problems.   _____

Try to be a good sport.   _____

Read the story below and then answer the questions.

When Andrew and Milly Jamison came home from school, they dropped
their coats and books on the living room floor. They were hungry and went
to the kitchen to get a snack. As they ate, they dropped crumbs on the floor
and spilled milk on the counter.

Milly told her brother to clean up the mess, but he left the kitchen and
slammed his bedroom door. Milly was shouting at Andrew and banging on
his bedroom door when their Mother arrived.

What do you think Mrs. Jamison should do? _____

_____

_____

Take this page home to share with your family.

Learning to get along with others
© 1990 by Incentive Publications, Inc., Nashville, TN.

Dear _____ ,

_____ is working on _____

_____ at school. You

can help _____ at home

by _____ . Please

call me at _____ , or write any comments or

suggestions you may have below and ask _____

to return the letter.

_____

_____

_____

_____

_____

Thanks for your help.

Date _____   Signature _____

CREATING THE "HEALTHFUL" CLASSROOM

Just For Teachers

A "healthful" classroom promotes the kind of environment in which children can learn and grow freely. The word "healthful" means many things and includes both physical and mental health. Read the checklist below and monitor yourself regularly to see if you are encouraging a healthful classroom. Add your own "rules and guidelines" to the list!

_____ Be a friend to all students. Personalities may clash on occasion, but always remember that you are the adult. An extra dose of friendship works miracles!

_____ Accept the feelings of *all* students. Try to learn about the homes from which the students come. You might be the only understanding adult a student has in his or her life.

_____ Always make the new student comfortable. Reach out!

_____ Avoid stress and pressure in your classroom. It can be felt by the students. Remember, tomorrow is another day — and there's always next week!

_____ Try not to show favoritism. Kids know who the "favorites" are, and they are hurt when they are not in that group.

_____ Positive reinforcement on a daily basis is a must, especially for the slow or learning disabled student. Praise is invaluable!

_____ Help your students to learn from their mistakes.

_____ Never ridicule or compare students in front of others. The damage is irreparable.

Try these ideas...

• Provide a few minutes each Friday for the students to write brief paragraphs noting problems they might have had during the week. Urge the students to ask for help when they need it.

• Create a "problem corner" in which you can meet with students on a voluntary basis. Personal or school difficulties can be discussed individually or in small groups. You may want to meet with particular students as necessary.

120

A telescope helps you to see things that are far away.

A telescope is made of curved glass and mirrors inside a long tube.

Have you ever used a telescope?

Make your own "telescope"!

1. Decorate a paper towel tube. Use crayons and markers to make it as fancy as you can!

2. When you have finished, go to a window in the classroom. Close one eye and look carefully through the tube with your other eye. Your telescope does not have the parts to make objects look closer, but it does help you to focus on one thing.

3. Select small objects and look at them through your telescope. When you find something you really like, study it carefully. Then write about that "thing." Describe the object carefully in the space provided on this page. Continue on the back of the page if you need more room.

<u>Description</u>

_____

_____

_____

_____

_____

_____

BLURBS-BLURBS-BLURBS

1. In a speech blurb like this I am talking.

Writing and drawing comic strips can be fun.

There are three different ways to write the "words" in a comic strip.

Draw your own comic strip below.

Then write the words for the comic strip!

In a funny one like this I am just thinking.

2.

In a box like this you can tell about what is going on. No one is talking or thinking now.

3.

The name of my comic is _____ .

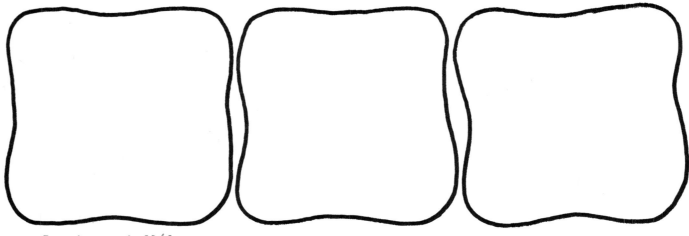

Learning to write blurbs

Name _____

PETS PETS PETS

HOW MANY DO WE HAVE?

A survey is useful for gathering all kinds of information.
Complete this survey to get to know your classmates better.
List the names of your classmates and the names of their pets on the chart below.

Classmates	Dogs	Cats	Fish	Birds	Other

1. How many dogs are listed? _____
2. How many cats are listed? _____
3. How many more dogs are listed than birds? _____
4. What is the total number of pets listed? _____
5. How many pets have the same name? _____

Learning to take a survey

DEAR PARENT,

can now

ISN'T THAT GREAT!

TEACHER

© 1990 by Incentive Publications, Inc., Nashville, TN.

DYNAMITE

Award presented to

_____

For _____

★ GREAT WORK ★

_____

TEACHER

Name _____

REBUS RECIPE

A rebus story has pictures or symbols in place of some of the words.
It looks like this:

Jamie — Lost And Found

Jamie was lost. She could not find the right  . She

did not see her . She sat down under a .

A small came along and licked her face with its big

 . The dog got her dirty. Jamie was

 when her came along and found her.

Use some of the symbols to the right to write your own rebus story.
Make up other symbols if you need them.

Write another story on the back of this page.
Cut tiny pictures out of magazines and paste them in place of
   some of the words.

Writing rebus stories
© 1990 by Incentive Publications, Inc., Nashville, TN.

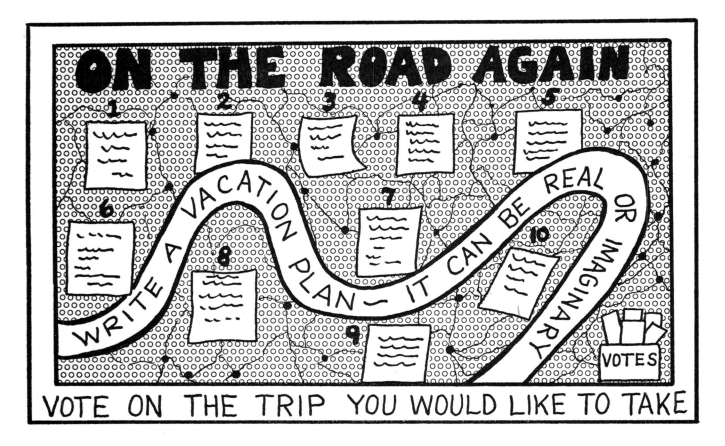

When the end of the school year approaches, it's time to take down bulletin boards. However, a gloomy room provides no inspiration for students. Try this idea...

Directions:
1. Cover a bulletin board with old road maps.
2. Write the caption "On The Road Again" with a bold marker.
3. Cut a "winding road" out of white butcher paper and write the following on it: "Write A Vacation Plan — It Can Be Real Or Imaginary." Attach the "road" to the board as shown.
4. Write the numbers 1–10 on the board.
5. Have each student write a paragraph or story detailing a summer trip (real or imaginary).
6. Tack ten of the completed stories on the board.
7. Give the students a few days to read all of the stories. Then, have each student vote on the trip he or she would like to take. (The students may place their ballots in a pocket on the board if desired.)
8. Repeat this procedure until all of the students' stories have been displayed on the board. Then display the "winning" trip stories on the board and have the class vote on the best trip of all.

SAFEGUARDING OUR ENVIRONMENT

Our landfills are overflowing, and we are "throwing away" products made from trees in our precious forests. The oceans and rivers are polluted; smog fills our air. We've endangered the lives of many of our animal friends; wildflowers are disappearing; the wetlands have been invaded; and there's a big hole in our sky. It's enough to make "Chicken Little" run and cover his head!

But, there's hope. The grass is still green and each morning the sun still rises. There are children in your classroom, and *you* have knowledge and vision. You are teaching a potential "army" of dedicated conservationists!

When using this chapter, we urge you to help the youngsters in your class to "experience" the earth's beauty and to prize it. They must treasure our natural resources and learn to use them wisely. Help them understand the vast problems that exist, but instill in them the understanding that through technology, political intervention, and a lot of hard work, we *will* survive and the world *will* be a better place. Come on out "Chicken Little", we'll make it OK!

In your students' lifetimes, half the earth's plants and animals may become extinct. They will best understand the meaning of "extinct" through the discussion of dinosaurs. Survival depends upon their understanding and future actions.

Bulletin Board Possibilities:
Find pictures of endangered species and mount them in "special frames." Use the board to display student work, findings, information, actions to take, etc.

TO MAKE SPECIAL FRAMES

1. Fold & Cut
2. Open up.
3. Glue or staple.

Alternative energy

Scientists are constantly searching for ways to harness the powers of the sun to replace the pollution emitting fossil fuels and nuclear energy.

Just For Teachers

Solar energy can be demonstrated to young children through the use of this simple experiment.

YOU WILL NEED:
1. One sunny window, shelf, or table.
2. Cookie sheet or tray.
3. Several small balls or marbles.
4. One short, thin candle (about three inches long).
5. Several books.
6. Magnifying glass.
7. A "prop" for the glass, e.g., clay or a juice can, filled with stones or sand.

DO THIS:
1. In a sunny window, prop one end of the cookie sheet up on the books.
2. Prop the other end on the top of the candle (adjust books to cookie sheet level).
3. Line the balls up on the tray.
4. Stand the magnifying glass up a short distance away.
5. Through the magnifying glass focus the sun on the candle.
6. Watch the powerful sun's rays slowly melt the wax and cause the balls to roll onto the floor.

HOORAY FOR THE SUN!

SEASONAL CRITTERS

You may want to trace or enlarge these whimsical animal friends. They will be great for bulletin boards, mobiles, notes to parents, invitations, student rewards, special assignments, student notepaper, etc.

Just For Teachers

summer

autumn

Just For Teachers

winter

Spring

131

Name _____

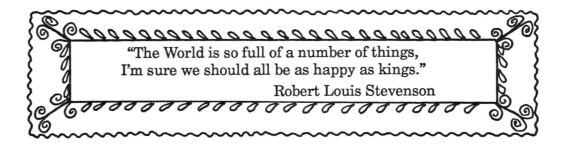

"The World is so full of a number of things,
I'm sure we should all be as happy as kings."
Robert Louis Stevenson

Beauty is all around us, but sometimes we do not take the time to see it. We must protect the beauty that we see, smell, hear, and feel so it will last.

Look up the meaning of the following words and write each in a sentence.

1. Environment _____

   _____

2. Conservation _____

   _____

3. Appreciation _____

   _____

4. Natural resources _____

   _____

Take this page outdoors or on a nature walk. Look and listen!
Fill in the boxes with beautiful things you find.

Share this with your family; together, add more words.

Name _____

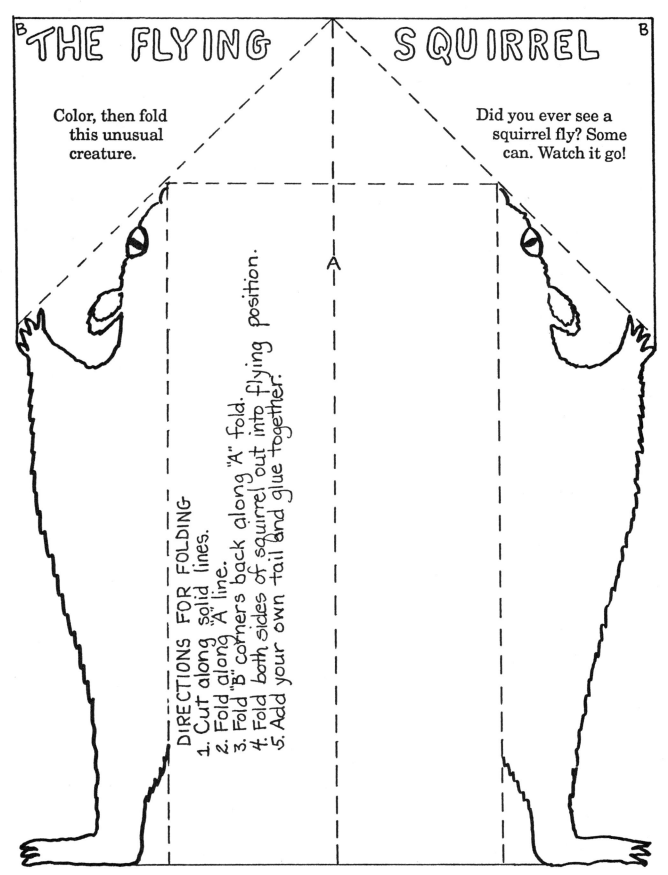

B THE FLYING SQUIRREL B

Color, then fold
this unusual
creature.

Did you ever see a
squirrel fly? Some
can. Watch it go!

A

DIRECTIONS FOR FOLDING
1. Cut along solid lines.
2. Fold along "A" line.
3. Fold "B" corners back along "A" fold.
4. Fold both sides of squirrel out into flying position.
5. Add your own tail and glue together.

WILLIE ~ The whale that lost its tail

Willie was a very unusual, giant, blue whale. He was always helping others who were sick or injured, but he only had half a tail. Use this space to tell *your* tale about how Willie lost *his* tail.

_____

_____

_____

_____

_____

_____

_____

_____

_____

_____

_____

_____

_____

_____

_____

_____

_____

Creative writing

Name _____

SAVE THE ROOS

The Australian kangaroo is a threatened species as they are hunted for their hides. Their environment is also changing.

This interesting animal is called a "marsupial." Marsupials have pouches where they keep their babies. Newborn kangaroos are only one inch long. They would be easy to lose if not kept in Mom's pocket. These healthy animals like to eat plants and vegetables and can live as long as fifteen years.

Kangaroos also are unique for their huge hind legs, big feet, and large tails. They use the legs to stand upright and to help them jump. They can hop great distances and when in a hurry can leap from five to twenty feet. Their long, powerful tails are used for balance and steering.

The great kangaroo is called a "forester" and can weigh 200 pounds, while the smaller "wallaby" is no bigger than a rabbit.

SAVE THE "ROOS"

Joey got lost in the outback. Can you help him get home safely?

*Answer Key

Learning about Kangaroos
© 1990 by INCENTIVE PUBLICATIONS, Inc., Nashville, TN.

Name _____

AIR EVERYWHERE

Environment is everything around us. The most important part of our environment is air. Air helps us in many ways.

Draw a line from the way air helps us to the picture of what it does. In each space, write the name of other things you can think of.

1. Air Works For Us

   _____

   _____

2. Air Fills Things

   _____

   _____

3. Air Moves Things

   _____

   _____

4. Air Pushes Things

   _____

   _____

5. All Living Things
   Need Air to Breathe

   _____

   _____

It is important that we keep our air clean. Can you tell why?

_____

Bring this page home; share it with your family.

Learning how air helps us
© 1990 by Incentive Publications, Inc., Nashville, TN.

Name _____

Clouds are beautiful.
We love to look at their different shapes. They are also very important as they give us the rain all living things need to grow. They also protect us from having too much sun.

Now Look At the Sky

• Can you find wispy clouds that look like feathers? They are "cirrus clouds."

• Can you find low, fluffy clouds that look like puffy pillows? They are called "cumulus clouds."

• Can you find great big piles of fluffy clouds? When they start turning dark in places they are called "thunderheads."

Use your cotton to make clouds in the sky patches.

FOR THIS ACTIVITY YOU WILL NEED:

1. Three small pieces of blue paper to paste on the sky patches
2. Several cotton balls and paste
3. One dark crayon
4. And one partly cloudy day

Learning cloud types
© 1990 by INCENTIVE PUBLICATIONS, Inc., Nashville, TN.

bits and pieces

FOR THE "LUNCH BUNCH" - Illustrate, then recycle lunch bags. Encourage students to use each for one week.

IT PAYS TO ADVERTISE - Make bumper stickers with new, creative slogans.

TAKE A STAND - Provide a weekly award for the student who demonstrates a concern for conservation. Have class vote to determine the winner. Present a special certificate.

AWARENESS: THE FIRST STEP - Foster student awareness through pictures, poetry, and nature walks. Encourage appreciation of the beauty surrounding us. Start a school beautification program! Make an "I Love" talking mural. Research tells us that a wall with a pretty painting on it is rarely the object of graffiti, a schoolyard with flowers surrounding it seldom trashed.

OUCH! IT HURTS - Discuss the importance of pitching in to help our world. Place a globe or global map in a prominent area of your room. Reserve time daily to tell of incidents students have seen or heard of that has "hurt" our world. Select one or two and have the students write a descriptive word on an adhesive bandage and place it anywhere on the map or globe. (Visual proof of our problems.)

ENVIRONMENTAL WREATH - Make a nature wreath for classroom or individual students. Cut a large cardboard "doughnut". Go for a nature walk, then have students glue the treasures they collected on the doughnut (dried weeds, leaves, acorns, pebbles, bark, moss, grass, etc.). Add a bright ribbon.

TRASHY WREATH - Kick off a school litter campaign with a huge wreath made from trash. Add a black bow! Display it in a prominent place in your building to stimulate interest.

SUGGESTIONS FOR BULLETIN BOARD USE:

This social and environmental concerns bulletin board could be a yearlong project. Current issues may be added or removed by writing them on separate slips of paper. Visual stimulation might be changed to enhance interest.

Student or group reports could be featured weekly in order to provide time for others to read the work. You may want to assign an art committee to coordinate the illustration with the current issue, or the student preparing the report can change the display by adding pictures and cutouts.

Make this bulletin board important! Encourage your students to make a careful choice, research the topic carefully, and take a stand. Find out what is happening on the local level – most importantly, what can *they* do! Ask the class to write suggestions for action and place them in the pocket.

Encourage students to demonstrate their concerns in some way – a letter-writing campaign, joining an organization, providing public information, starting an antilittering work force, or raising money to fight for the "cause" can *all* make a difference!

THE CHALLENGE OF CONSERVATION <u>MUST</u> BEGIN AT AN EARLY AGE IN ORDER TO PROVIDE A SAFE WORLD FOR FUTURE GENERATIONS!

Conservation bulletin board
© 1990 by Incentive Publications, Inc., Nashville, TN.

Name _____

BE THE SOLUTION - NOT THE CAUSE

Did you know that every three months United States consumers throw away enough aluminum to rebuild our commercial fleet of airplanes? Did you know that every two weeks we discard enough bottles to fill the 1,350 feet twin towers of the New York World Trade Center? Wow!

What is your family throwing away or recycling? Keep track for a week. Post this sheet in the kitchen and ask all household members to make a small check (✓) in the correct container each time an item is trashed (or recycled).

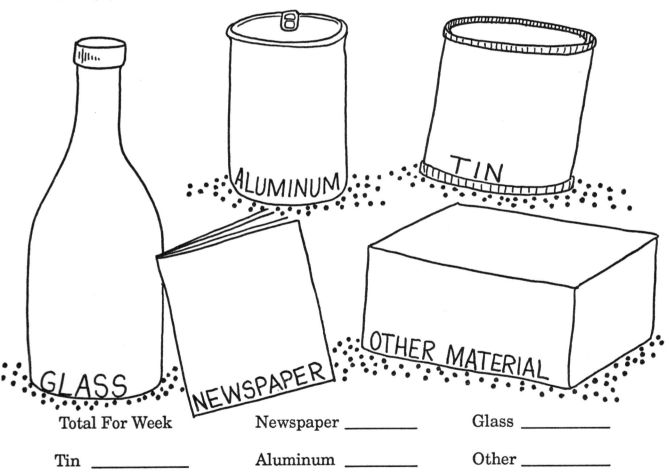

Total For Week

Newspaper _____   Glass _____

Tin _____   Aluminum _____   Other _____

If your community does not have a recycling program, start collecting. Bring your trash to a disposal center. You may even find a place that pays "cash for trash"! Go one step further — try "garbage prevention." Ask your Mom to buy <u>ONLY</u> things that can be recycled! Recycling pays off!

Demonstrating recycling awareness
© 1990 by Incentive Publications, Inc., Nashville, TN.

PANDA PUZZLER

Pandas look like giant, cuddly, black-eyed teddy bears that have come to life. Their natural habitat is the mountains of China. They eat bamboo while sitting up like humans.

Pandas are mysterious creatures. It is thought they are related to racoons, not the bears they resemble.

One of the most famous pandas is Ling Ling who was given to our country by China. She lives in the National Zoo in Washington, D.C. Ling Ling is very bashful but playful. She is a happy panda.

We hope the natural habitat of the panda does not change so that these lovable but puzzling animals will be around for a long time.

H	B	A	M	B	O	O	O
A	P	C	H	Z	O	O	O
B	A	C	I	M	C	P	P
I	N	H	B	E	A	R	R
T	D	I	A	W	L	D	D
A	A	N	I	M	A	L	L
T	R	A	C	O	O	N	N

Find the puzzle words in the story and underline them!

Panda word maze
© 1990 by Incentive Publications, Inc., Nashville, TN.

141

*Answer Key

Name _____

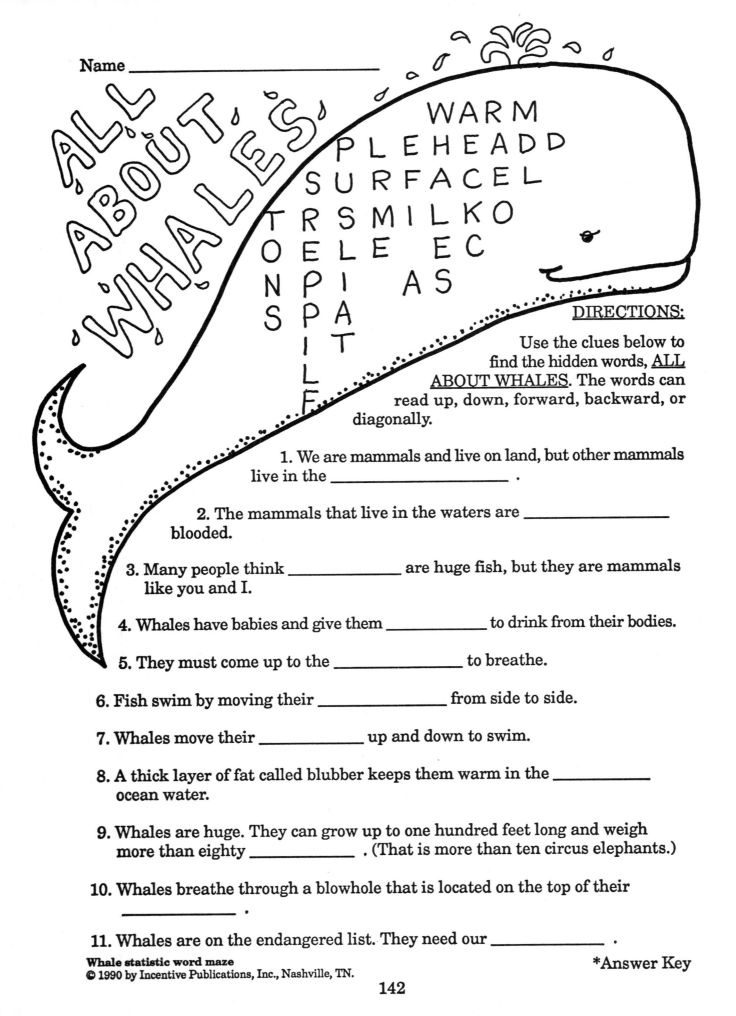

ALL ABOUT WHALES

```
                    W A R M
            P L E H E A D D
          S U R F A C E L
    T   R S M I L K O
    O   E L E   E C
    N   P I     A S
    S   P A
        I T
        L
        F
```

DIRECTIONS:

Use the clues below to find the hidden words, ALL ABOUT WHALES. The words can read up, down, forward, backward, or diagonally.

1. We are mammals and live on land, but other mammals live in the _____ .

2. The mammals that live in the waters are _____ blooded.

3. Many people think _____ are huge fish, but they are mammals like you and I.

4. Whales have babies and give them _____ to drink from their bodies.

5. They must come up to the _____ to breathe.

6. Fish swim by moving their _____ from side to side.

7. Whales move their _____ up and down to swim.

8. A thick layer of fat called blubber keeps them warm in the _____ ocean water.

9. Whales are huge. They can grow up to one hundred feet long and weigh more than eighty _____ . (That is more than ten circus elephants.)

10. Whales breathe through a blowhole that is located on the top of their _____ .

11. Whales are on the endangered list. They need our _____ .

Whale statistic word maze
© 1990 by Incentive Publications, Inc., Nashville, TN.

*Answer Key

Name ______________________________

LITTER hunt

WHAT SHOULD GO IN THE TRASH?

BE A HELPER! CLEAN UP YOUR ENVIRONMENT!

Directions - Look on the trash can to find the word for each picture. Write the word on the line to match the picture.

If you think it should be thrown in the trash, draw a big arrow from that word to the trash can.

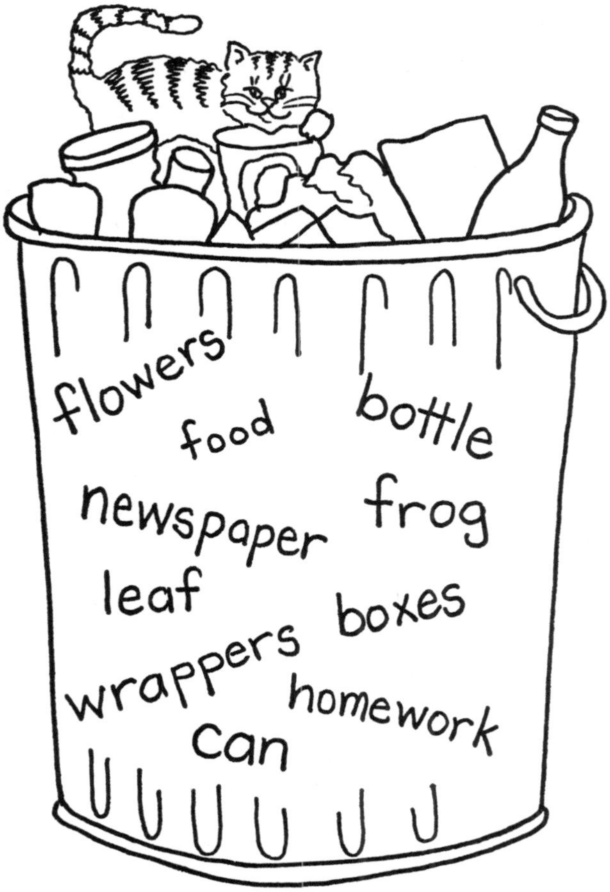

flowers
food
bottle
newspaper
frog
leaf
boxes
wrappers
homework
can

BE A HELPER! PICK UP TRASH! LITTER POLLUTES!

1. ______________________

2. ______________________

3. ______________________

4. ______________________

5. ______________________

6. ______________________

7. ______________________

8. ______________________

9. ______________________

10. ______________________

Developing litter awareness

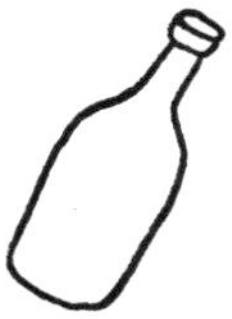

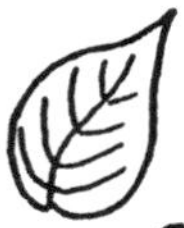

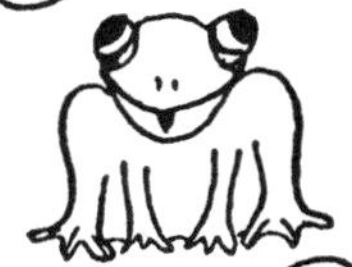

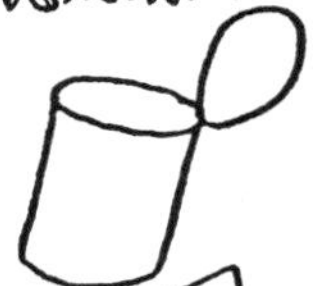

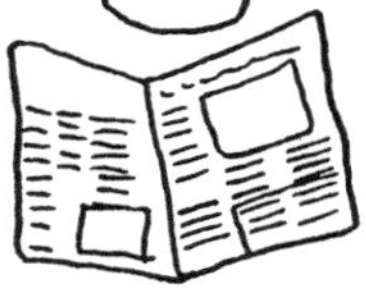

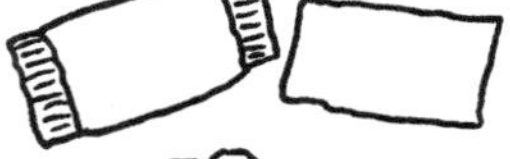

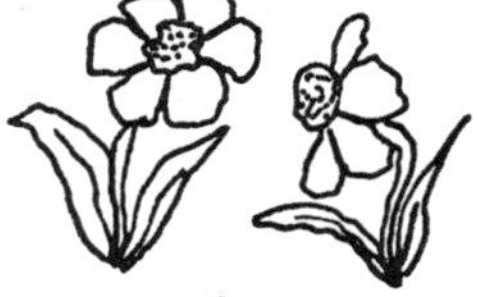

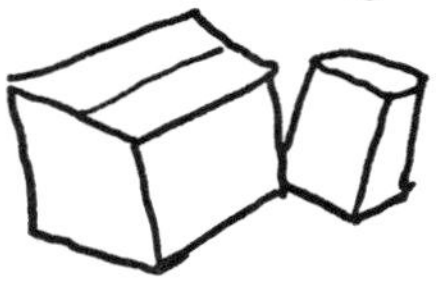

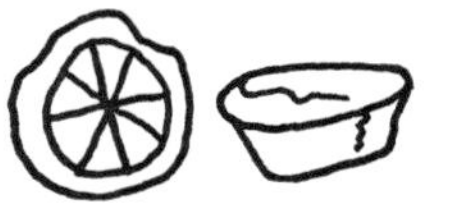

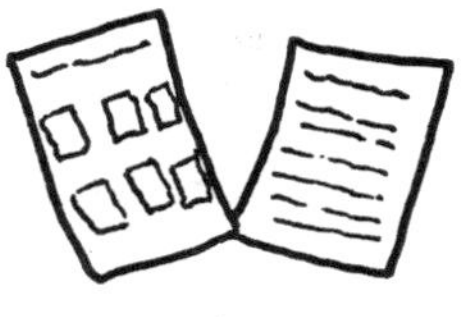

Name _____

STOP! YOU ARE HURTING MY WORLD

Because certain wild animals provide useful materials as well as trophies, they are being destroyed very quickly. Furs, ivory, horns, skins, feathers, oils, and even meat provide dollars for poachers. Sport for game hunters is also a threat to these animals. Many are in danger of becoming extinct.

Change in their living environment is also a threat to many species of animals. Drought, pollution, disappearance of plant life on which animals feed, growth of cities, and cutting down forests are just a few of the dangers to our wildlife.

Once a species of animals become extinct, there is no way to ever get it back. Conservation and protection are the only hopes for the future.

The U.S. Fish and Wildlife Service, The National Wildlife Federation, and Greenpeace are just a few of the many organizations concerned with conservation.

Check the animals you know about.

Sea Otter ❑
Crocodile ❑
Panda ❑
Polar Bear ❑
Seal ❑
Penguin ❑
Elephant ❑
Florida Panther ❑
Osprey ❑
Bald Eagle ❑
Sea Turtle ❑
Grizzly Bear ❑
Dolphin ❑
Chimpanzee ❑
Whale ❑
_____ ❑
(other)

DO THIS:

Select one of the endangered or threatened species from this partial list and find out its current status. Is there any way you can support the actions being taken? Write about your findings on the back of this page.

Learning about endangered or threatened species
© 1990 by Incentive Publications, Inc., Nashville, TN.

Today's popular media is bringing "to life" the day-to-day struggles of the earth's sea mammals. Your students should be well aware of the conservationists and the organizations working toward the survival of endangered and threatened species.

Be sure they know the terms! "Endangered" - animals that are currently in danger of becoming extinct. "Threatened" - animals that are likely to become endangered in the foreseeable future. Once an animal is designated "endangered", it may not be bought, sold, collected, harmed, or killed.

Many zoos and aquariums across the country have adoption programs that are inexpensive. Most animals are named, have a brief biography, and can be selected through photos. Your local zoo may have a program where they sell shares in order to provide feed and care. This can be a great way for your students to feel involved in a "humanitarian act." Hold a class fund-raiser to raise the money needed. Get involved!

You or your students may want to write for information to one of the following organizations.

Adopt
The Philadelphia Zoo
34th and Girard
Philadelphia, PA 19104

Save The Manatee Club
1101 Audubon Way
Mainland, FL 32751

Adopt an Audubon Animal
P.O. Box 4237
New Orleans, LA 70178

Whale Adoption Project
P.O. Box 316-N
Woods Hole, MA 02543

You may want to look in your yellow pages for a local zoo, nature conservancy, or game preserve.

Name _____

aquarium antics

All living things need a special habitat. Color the pictures that you think belong in the aquarium. Cut them out and paste them in the fish tank. You may want to draw more.

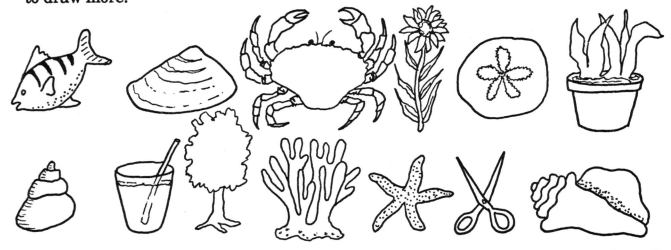

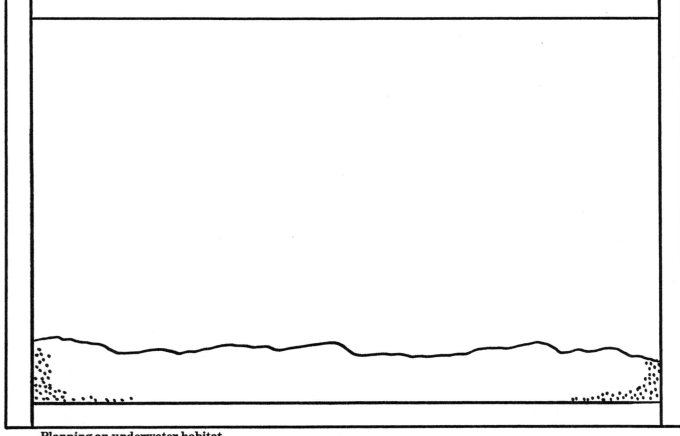

AN UNDERWATER HABITAT

TRASHY STORY

Trash disposal is a serious problem. Find out more about one of the topics listed below, then finish the story about Tom.

Continue your story on the back of this page.

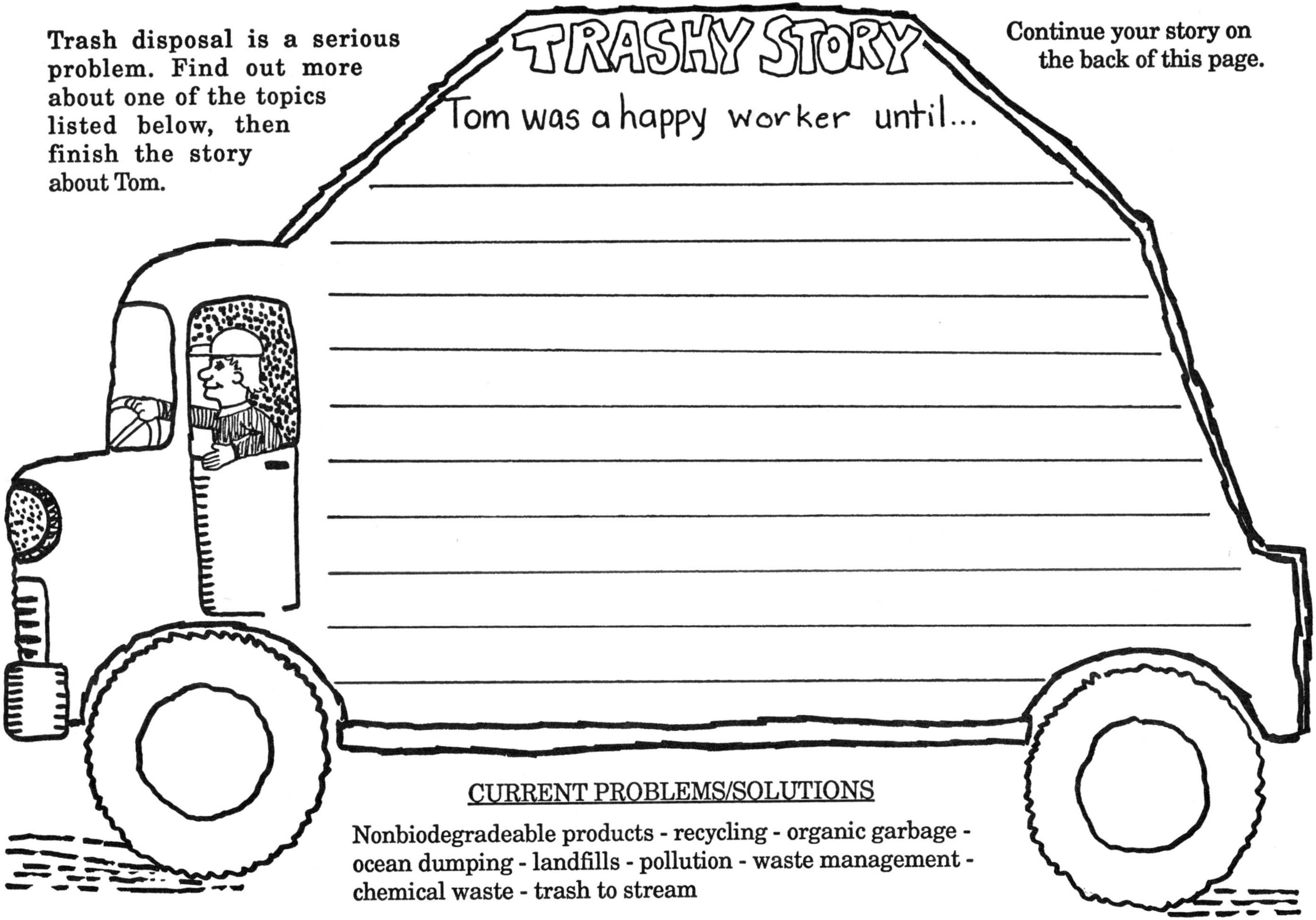

Tom was a happy worker until...

_____
_____
_____
_____
_____
_____
_____
_____
_____
_____
_____
_____
_____

CURRENT PROBLEMS/SOLUTIONS

Nonbiodegradeable products - recycling - organic garbage - ocean dumping - landfills - pollution - waste management - chemical waste - trash to stream

Learning about the problems of trash disposal
© 1990 by Incentive Publications, Inc, Nashville, TN.

Name _____

Where have they gone?

All Living Things Need a Special Environment

Find the six hidden creatures on the land that need water to live in.

Find the six hidden things in the water that need the land to live on. List them below:

Needs Land		Needs Water	
1._____	4._____	1._____	4._____
2._____	5._____	2._____	5._____
3._____	6._____	3._____	6._____

Identifying the special needs of living things

Name _____

Some creatures make you smile

Some creatures can help us. List the ones you can think of.

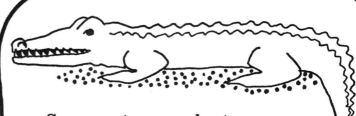

Some creatures can hurt us. List the ones you can think of.

Some creatures are just fun and make us smile. List the ones you like.

Some creatures need our help. You may have an S.P.C.A., a nature conservancy, or game preserve near you. Use this space to write how you think they can help or how *you* can help our animal friends.

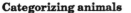

Categorizing animals

OUR PROTECTORS

Hundreds of nonprofit organizations are working to promote environmental awareness. Some are educational and scientific for the purpose of understanding conservation. Others take action!

We have provided a partial list which may be useful for letter-writing, class projects, or background information. A complete conservation directory may be obtained from the National Wildlife Federation, 1400 Tenth Street, N.W., Washington, D.C. 20036.

Acid Rain Information Clearinghouse
33 South Washington Street
Rochester, NY 14608

Air Pollution Control Association
P.O. Box 2861
Pittsburgh, PA 15230

American Humane Association
9725 East Hampden
Denver, CO 80231

American Association of Zoo Keepers
635 Gage Boulevard
Topeka, KS 66606

Arctic Institute of North America
2500 University Drive, N.W.
Calgary, Alberta CANADA T2N N4

Children of the Green Earth
P.O. Box 95219
Seattle, WA 98145

Clean Water Action Project
317 Pennsylvania Avenue S.E., Suite 200
Washington, D.C. 20003

The Cousteau Society
930 West 21st Street
Norfolk, VA 23517

American Conservation Association, Inc.
30 Rockefeller Plaza
Room 5510
New York, NY 10020

Defenders of Wildlife
1244 19th Street, N.W.
Washington, D.C. 20036

The Eagle Foundation
P.O. Box 155
Apple River, IL 61001

Elsa Wild Animal Appeal, U.S.A.
P.O. Box 4572
North Hollywood, CA 91607

Greenpeace, U.S.A.
1436 U Street, N.W.
Washington, DC 20009

American Forestry Association
1516 P Street, N.W.
Washington, DC 20036

Worldwatch Institute
1776 Massachusetts Avenue, N.W.
Washington, DC 20036

National Trappers Association
P.O. Box 3667
Bloomington, IL 61702

National Audubon Society
950 Third Avenue
New York, NY 10022

Desert Protective Council
P.O. Box 4294
Palm Springs, CA 92263

Puppetry is fun! It's an escape from realism and can spark your daily activities. Even the shy child comes to life when speaking words through another image.

Select plan "A" or "B" for making your easy, reversible "puppet mitt."

Plan A

- Make a pattern for student use
- Run dittos or provide carbon for copying
- Color features and cut out shapes
- Glue around edge, or punch holes and lace

Plan B

- Use carbon to trace on burlap or other fabric
- Use felt pen to outline features
- Stitch around edge by hand or machine

SUGGESTIONS FOR USE:

1. Make one puppet for sharing, or provide time for students to make individual copies.

2. Have students search through newspaper for environmental articles. Pass Sal/Sam around for individual readings. Very young students can tell about an article that has been read to them at home.

3. Look through magazines for pictures of animals. Have each student select one to share with class. Use Sal or Sam to share feelings about the picture.

4. Make a list of possible environmental concerns, solutions, or actions. Read each aloud and have class "vote" on the issue of statement using their puppets, e.g., "I saw someone throw a newspaper in the trash basket this morning." (vote) "I took it out to recycle it." (vote)

5. Make up timely lyrics to familiar children's tunes with your students. Have your "puppet chorus" sing for other classrooms.

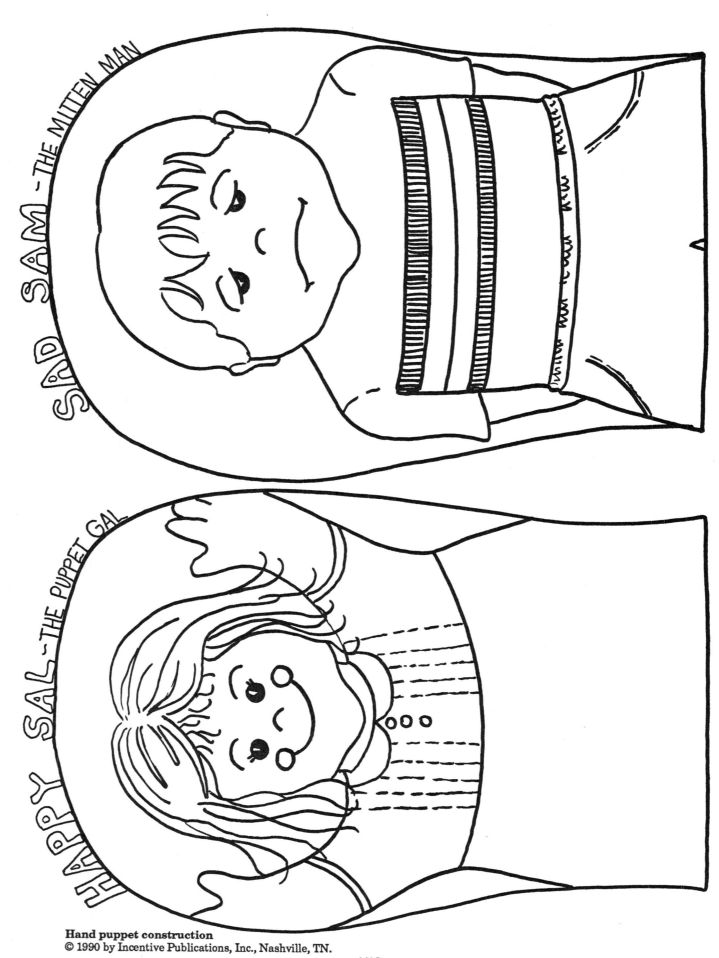

SAD SAM – THE MITTEN MAN

HAPPY SAL – THE PUPPET GAL

Hand puppet construction
© 1990 by Incentive Publications, Inc., Nashville, TN.

Name _____

Read "Our Green Poem," then write your own. Remember, poems do not have to rhyme!

Our Green Poem   Your Green Poem

                                  _____

Green is for grass,   _____
The leaf and the tree.
                                  _____

Green is for pasture   _____
As far as we see.
                                  _____

Green is for mountains   _____
That rise from the sea.
                                  _____

Green is my world -   _____
Protect it for me!
                                  _____

MAKE A PICTURE OF YOUR FAVORITE GREEN PLACE

SHARE THIS WITH YOUR FAMILY

Fostering nature appreciation
© 1990 by Incentive Publications, Inc., Nashville, TN.

Name _____

WILDERNESS CONQUEST

Directions:

1. Take turns rolling a die.
2. Move the number of spaces shown on die.
3. Pick a card and read aloud.
4. Follow the directions.
5. Return card to bottom of pack.

Climb the mountain and return safely!

You will need!
- Two markers
- One friend
- Game cards
- A die

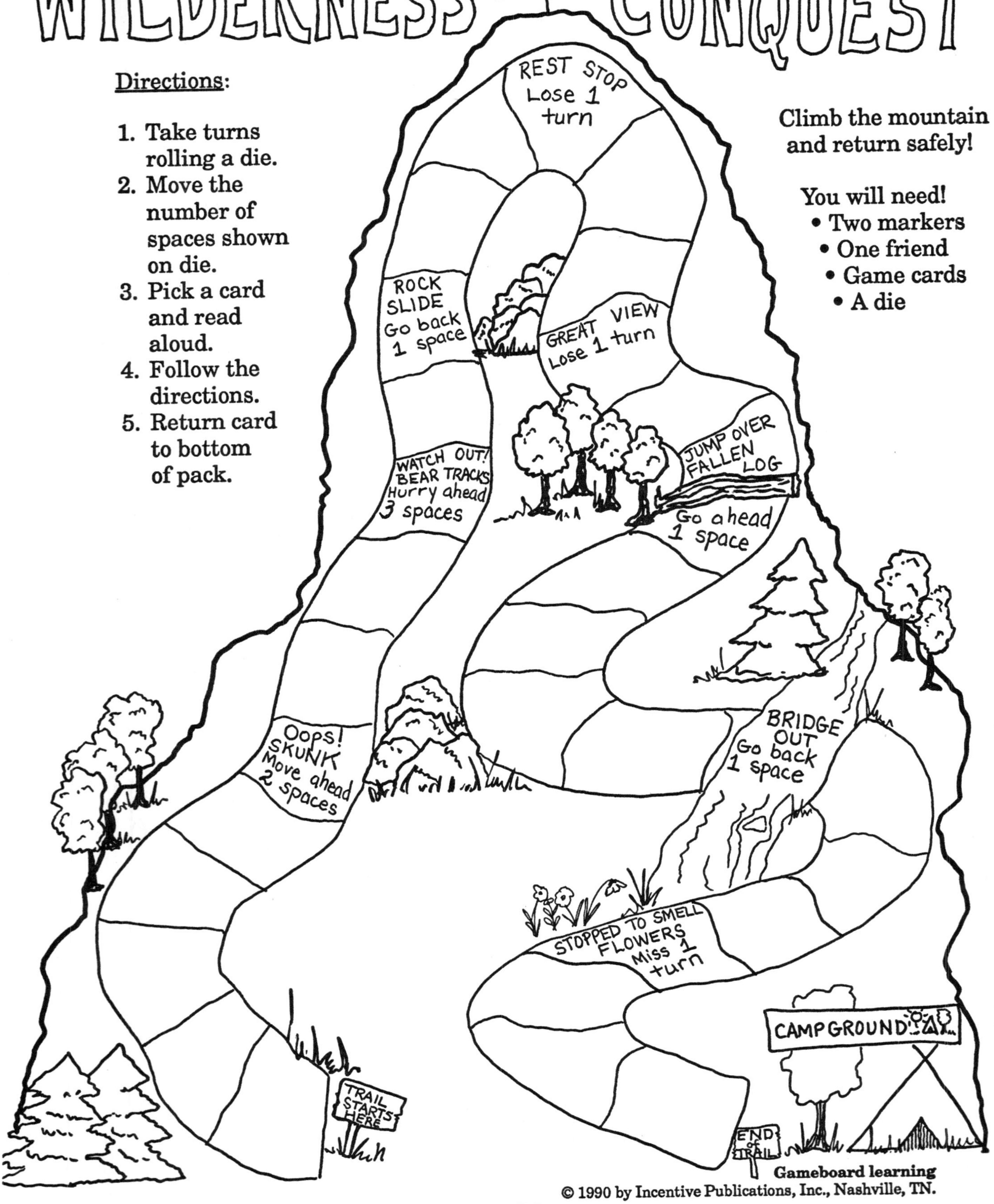

REST STOP
Lose 1 turn

ROCK SLIDE
Go back 1 space

GREAT VIEW
Lose 1 turn

JUMP OVER FALLEN LOG
Go ahead 1 space

WATCH OUT!
BEAR TRACKS
Hurry ahead 3 spaces

BRIDGE OUT
Go back 1 space

OOPS!
SKUNK
Move ahead 2 spaces

STOPPED TO SMELL FLOWERS
Miss 1 turn

CAMPGROUND

TRAIL STARTS HERE

END OF TRAIL

Gameboard learning

© 1990 by Incentive Publications, Inc., Nashville, TN.

SHUTTLING ABOVE AND ABOUT

Man has been living the dream of space exploration for many years. The excitement, the glory, the awe-inspiring achievements are still a part of that dream. How far can we go? What will we learn to help mankind?

A new flight is leaving Kennedy Space Center. You are one of the astronauts. Name your ship, get out your stellar map, and blast off. Use this page as the launching pad for *your* story!

_____

_____

_____

_____

_____

_____

_____

_____

_____

_____

_____

Super challenge writing composition
© 1990 by Incentive Publications, Inc., Nashville, TN.

GLITTER- don't LITTER

Encourage your students to notice litter, find ways to clean up their environment, and to take action. Make up slogans together. Make copies of the patterns to write on. Distribute slogans at home, public places, or use as refrigerator memos or on bulletin boards. Add a touch of glitter!

HEADWORK and FOOTWORK

Pollution makes our air dirty. It can hurt your entire breathing system. It can also make your nose run, eyes burn, throat sore, and make you cough.

It can damage your lungs, heart, and other organs. We breathe much easier when we do not have dirty air in our environment.

Check out your environment!

Find out how much air pollution you may be breathing.

<u>You will need:</u>

• petroleum jelly
• several 3" x 5" cards
• pencil and tape
• you may want a helper

<u>POSSIBLE LOCATIONS</u>

<u>DO THIS</u>:

1. Put today's date on each card.
2. Find places where you think there is dirty air.
3. Tape a card to that spot.
4. Smear some petroleum jelly on the card.
5. Leave the card overnight.
6. Check the card the next day. Describe what you see on the petroleum jelly. How are the areas different?

WHAT ARE WE BREATHING?

your garage

in a smoker's room

school boiler room

school hall

school windowsill

your bedroom

Science experiment-discovering sources of pollution

Name _____

making FOG and SMOG

Fog happens.
Smog happens because we make it happen. Help your students understand the difference and be aware of the potential dangers.

Demonstration A

To make fog you will need a large jug and a cork with a hole in it. Wash out the jug with warm water leaving moisture on the inside. Insert the stopper and blow air into the hole. Quickly cover the hole to keep the air inside. When you remove the cork, a small "cloud" (or fog) will appear inside the jug.

Note: Clouds form when moisture and warm air meet with cooler air.

Demonstration B

Repeat the procedure. Before you insert the cork, drop in a lighted match. Insert the cork and blow in air; quickly remove the cork. You will observe thick fog.

*Note: When mixed with smoke, fog becomes smog.

BE SURE YOUR STUDENTS UNDERSTAND THAT IT IS HARMFUL TO OUR BODIES TO BREATHE SMOG. Ask them to look for smog in their environment. Make a class list. Take action!

WILDERNESS CONQUEST

An indoor, "outdoor" game to reinforce positive behavior!

<u>Directions</u>: Cut out the game cards below. You may want to add your own math facts, spelling words, other skill to be learned on the back, or use as is. Cut 3" x 5" index cards to make additional game cards. Add your own rules.

Never feed wild animals	Do not damage plants or trees	Always pick up your trash
Move one space	Move one space	Move two spaces
You did not put out your campfire	Leave wild animals alone	You picked wildflowers
Go back two spaces	Do not move	Go back one space
Never walk off alone	Always carry a water supply	Never eat wild berries
Do not move	Move one space	Do not move
Reward - take two turns	Do not litter — Move one space	Follow directions ranger may give you — Move two spaces

Variety gameboard cards
© 1990 by Incentive Publications, Inc., Nashville, TN.

ANSWER KEY

Pg. 12   1) children at play 2) no bicycle riding 3) no right turns 4) no campfires

Pg. 18   1) #2 jumps to #1 2) #4 jumps to #2 3) #7 jumps to #4 4) #3 jumps to #7
         5) #6 jumps to #3 6) #2 jumps to #6 7) #5 jumps to #2 8) #1 jumps to #5

Pg. 20   1) reptiles 2) hippos 3) bear cave 4) petting zoo 5) giraffes 6) right 7) right

Pg. 41   1) 5 2) Yes — He had been packing the car for hours and he had a headache.
         3) Yes — They were excited about the trip. 4) tuna sandwiches and fruit
         5) They heard a dog barking and followed the sound. 6) He was happy.

Pg. 43   1) make-believe 2) real 3) real 4) make-believe

Pg. 54   1) 2:25 2) 11:30 3) 5:15 4) bedtime 5) 8:30

Pg. 55   1) $.03 2) $.04 3) $.05 4) $.05 5) $.06 6) $.23

Pg. 57   You are smart.

Pg. 59
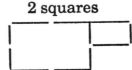

Pg. 61 / Pg. 65
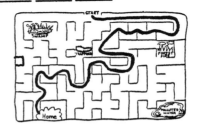

Pg. 67   1) $1.20 2) $4.00 3) $10.00 4) $4.70 5) Winesap — $2.40 6) will vary
         7) $22.30 plus answer to #6

Pg. 70   1) 6 C brown sugar; 2 C milk; 9 tbs. butter; 3 C chopped nuts; 1 1/2 tsp. vanilla
         2) 1/2 C brown sugar; 1/6 C milk; 3/4 tbs. butter; 1/4 C chopped nuts; 1/8 tsp.
vanilla

Pg. 72   1) 444 + 444 + 44 + 44 + 4 + 4 + 4 + 4 + 4 + 4 = 1000 2) 19 hours
         3) original figure   2 squares   3 squares   4) 100 nickels

Pg. 92

Pg. 135

Pg. 141   panda
bear
habitat
China
bamboo
racoons
zoo
animals

Pg. 142
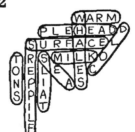

   1) sea   7) flippers
   2) warm   8) cold
   3) whales   9) tons
   4) milk   10) head
   5) surface 11) help
   6) tails